The Power of
Project-Based Learning

The Power of Project-Based Learning

Helping Students Develop Important Life Skills

Scott D. Wurdinger

ROWMAN & LITTLEFIELD
Lanham • Boulder • New York • London

Published by Rowman & Littlefield
A wholly owned subsidiary of The Rowman & Littlefield Publishing Group, Inc.
4501 Forbes Boulevard, Suite 200, Lanham, Maryland 20706
www.rowman.com

Unit A, Whitacre Mews, 26-34 Stannary Street, London SE11 4AB

British Library Cataloguing in Publication Information Available

Library of Congress Cataloging-in-Publication Data Available

ISBN 978-1-4758-2764-4 (cloth : alk. paper)
ISBN 978-1-4758-2765-1 (pbk : alk. paper)
ISBN 978-1-4758-2766-8 (electronic)

♾™ The paper used in this publication meets the minimum requirements of
American National Standard for Information Sciences—Permanence of Paper
for Printed Library Materials, ANSI/NISO Z39.48-1992.

Printed in the United States of America

Contents

Figures

Tables

Preface

When I graduated from high school, my guidance counselor told me that I was not smart enough to attend a four-year college and instead I should think about working in the trades or attending a junior college. Most of my high school courses were taught using the lecture method followed by standardized tests. Luckily I had one instructor who taught experientially, and it was in this course that I excelled. The only academic content I remember from high school centered on a project I completed in this course.

The instructor of this environmental education course encouraged me to attend a four-year college, and so I did. There are many students today, like me, who are told they are not smart enough to attend a four-year institution because they have low test scores. There are many people who learn best through direct experience, and I wrote this book for those individuals. I would argue that includes most of us.

My entire career has focused on inspiring students and faculty to become experiential educators, using approaches such as project-based learning to motivate and engage their own students in learning. My life's calling has been to encourage people to use these types of approaches because they work. I've seen many students over the years become extremely excited about creating a project on their own because it had meaning and purpose to their life at the time.

It took me eight years to finish my undergraduate degree—not because I did poorly in my classes, but because I was bored with the courses that were heavily laden with the lecture method. I would attend for a year, read about something exciting and interesting, and set out to experience firsthand what I was reading. My parents thought I was crazy when I came home one day and told them that I was dropping out of college and moving to Ely, Minnesota, to trap timber wolves for the US Fish and Wildlife Service.

My firsthand experiences were extremely engaging and exciting, and I was depressed when I returned to college to resume the same process of sitting in classes, taking notes, memorizing information, and taking exams. In my gut I knew this was not the way students should be educated: they should be out of the classroom, experiencing things firsthand, which inspires and motivates them to learn.

Reading and memorizing information about what others had already discovered was not engaging for me. Contacting a wolf researcher and acquiring a job trapping wolves to conduct research was engaging. This was my pattern for eight years: go to college for a year, read and memorize information for exams, and then take a year off and set out to experience what I had been reading.

On a visceral level I realized that direct experience was much more inspiring because the learning was deep and rich. I remember very little about the books I read as an undergraduate biology student, but I can show you precisely how to set a number-fourteen leg-hold trap to catch a timber wolf to this day, and that was something I did back in 1979.

My time away from school was filled with experiences like trapping and radio collaring timber wolves, working as a naturalist at a nature center, and helping organize and instruct adventure trips for organizations such as Outward Bound and the Prairie Mountaineers. What resulted was learning that was meaningful and relevant to my life at that point.

The skills I learned went far beyond academic content and technical skills. I learned how to communicate, problem solve, manage my time, be responsible for my actions, and collaborate with peers. These skills were invaluable, and I owe these *out-of-school experiences* to learning life skills that I continue to use to this day.

I realized through my own life's journey that writing a book like this will help educators understand how to implement this approach in their classes and will ultimately help students save time and money by experiencing their interests while in school rather than having to leave school to do so. Allowing students to create worthwhile projects will inspire them to stay in school and will allow them to learn important life skills needed for when they enter the work world.

The time is ripe for colleges and schools to incorporate more project-based learning in their curricula. While researching this book, I came across numerous articles analyzing a variety of educational benefits that result from using this approach. The research was overwhelming as to how project-based learning improves things such as self-confidence, problem solving, critical thinking, creativity, communication, collaboration, and time management, as well as understanding the academic content of the course in which students are enrolled.

This book is timely because a number of research studies have identified pertinent life skills needed at the workplace that have been shown to be enhanced and developed by project-based learning.

There is also a gap in the literature with books on project-based learning for higher education. There are plenty of books written for K–12 educators but none that I have found specifically for higher-education instructors. There are many research studies analyzing project-based learning in college classes, so it is obvious that instructors are using it at this level, where, results show, it works. But very few, if any, books have been written on the topic. My hope is that this book will fill that gap.

Acknowledgments

There are many people I need to thank for their help in pulling this book together. First, I thank my wife, Annette, and my daughters, Madeline and Lauren. They gave me my space and uninterrupted time to write this book. My wife drove many of the long trips to Iowa and Wisconsin to visit family while I pounded away on my laptop. My daughters helped me when I had questions about how to more efficiently use Microsoft Word.

Doug Thomas, Dee Thomas, and Ron Newell were some of the pioneers in Minnesota who took the theories behind project-based learning and implemented them at the charter school they created—Minnesota New Country School in Henderson, Minnesota. The first year of operation was 1994, and since that time the school has been visited by hundreds of educators from around the world, intrigued by how this approach is being implemented at this school. Thomas, Thomas, and Newell inspired me to learn about this approach and conduct research at their project-based learning schools. Without them, this book would have never been written.

Thanks to Innovative Quality Schools, and in particular Bob Wedl, Jerry Robicheau, and Phil Moye, for inviting me to be a cadre expert in the organization and to oversee charter schools using project-based learning. My experience with this organization has allowed me to visit project-based schools throughout Minnesota and interview staff and students about their experiences there.

All of the graduate students I have had in my courses over the years at Minnesota State University have helped me form my thinking on project-based learning. My seminar courses provide opportunities for students to critique my theories and teaching approaches, and their questions aided me in developing my thoughts for this book.

I owe a very special thanks to one of our current doctoral assistants—
Megan Weerts—who did an outstanding job reviewing in-text citations and
references to ensure they were properly formatted. She spent numerous hours
helping me in this endeavor.

I also offer a very special thank-you to Kellian Klink, library research
specialist at Minnesota State University, Mankato. I often conducted online
library searches for articles on very specific topics, and Kellian was always
able to locate and send me pertinent information, much of which is cited in
this book. She rose to the occasion many times, sometimes on holidays, and
her insights on how to conduct these searches were invaluable. Without her
help I would not have found many of these articles.

I thank Dr. Jean Haar, dean of the College of Education at Minnesota
State University, for allowing me to take a sabbatical so that I could begin
the process of writing this book. I was able to conduct much of the research
and write half the book during that semester. She has always been extremely
supportive of my research agenda.

Dr. Candace Raskin, current chair of the Department of Educational Leadership at Minnesota State University, Mankato, also signed off on my sabbatical and was very supportive of my time away from the department while
I worked on this book. I thank her for being very excited and energetic about
my research agenda.

I thank my research partner, Walter Enloe, who is Gordon B. Sanders Chair
in the School of Education at Hamline University in Saint Paul, Minnesota.
Walter and I have conducted several research projects together and have a
strong affiliation toward project-based learning. He has done remarkable
work in this area and has mentored many graduate students over the years,
encouraging them to use this approach in their own teaching.

Carrie Bakken is program coordinator at Avalon Charter School in Saint
Paul, Minnesota, and has helped support our research agenda by providing
access to students at her school. Her constant willingness to help us out and
make things happen with our research was incredibly valuable. She is a stal-
wart supporter of project-based learning and has been referenced in several
books for all her efforts in moving the field's efforts forward.

I thank Julie Carlson, my colleague, who was always available to answer
my questions about various things such as citation formatting and topic
progression. She is a fantastic office suitemate and is incredibly kind and
thoughtful to all who enter her office.

Dan Swenson, former student in the Experiential Education Graduate
Program, provided a thorough proofread of the entire book and found many
typos that spellcheck did not. He spent several days carefully proofing each
chapter, which is greatly appreciated.

I thank Mariam Qureshi, former doctoral student, who assisted me in a research project looking at graduate student life skills development during a semester-long course. Our research is referenced in chapter 3, where readers can see a chart that Mariam created while doing our research. Her help with the research was invaluable.

Finally, I thank Anahit Apinyan and Arynn Martin, who assisted me in creating several of the tables and figures in this book. Anahit and Arynn were graduate assistants for Academic Technology Services at Minnesota State University. What they created in a matter of an hour or less would have taken me all day. They were wonderful students to work with and were quick to capture the concepts we discussed for the graphics.

Introduction

The seven chapters to this book are organized in a sequence that moves from theory to practice. Chapter 1 provides readers with an argument for why education needs to change from a passive to an active process in the classroom. Lessons are borrowed from the business world that show how motivation and purpose are missing from the field of education.

The current education system relies heavily on lecture and test taking, but students are bored and apathetic with this approach. Motivation and inspiration are by-products of project-based learning, because students enjoy creating products relevant and meaningful to them.

Chapter 2 begins by providing readers with a definition of *project-based learning* and discusses its historical roots. Surprisingly, the project method has been around for a long time, going back to the late 1800s when the Massachusetts Institute for Technology began using projects in their engineering courses. Later, in 1918, William Kilpatrick, student of John Dewey, wrote the article "The Project Method."

Many administrators want proof that a new approach to learning is effective, so I provide a variety of research articles proving the method works at the K–12 and collegiate levels. This section reads a little like a literature review, but it identifies a number of research articles educators can use as evidence that project-based learning works and that they can share with their administrators.

There are several teaching approaches to experiential learning that are explained in this chapter, as well as discussions as to how educators can infuse project-based learning in all of these approaches. The chapter then considers what preparation this approach entails. Finally, the chapter closes by explaining the potential problems educators may face while implementing this approach.

Chapter 3 explains and defines the term *life skills* and argues that life skills development, promoted by a number of scholars, must be integrated into educators' teaching. I list eight particular life skills of relevance to this book.

Personal stories of students who have developed these life skills are offered, as is as an explanation for why life skills development is a slow process that occurs over a long period of time. Multiple research studies mentioned in this chapter make it quite evident that project-based learning allows students to develop these eight different life skills.

Chapter 4 is very practical, providing the reader a number of projects conducted by my students over the years. These projects are discussed in detail so that readers can incorporate them into their own curricula.

In addition, examples are provided in which students have networked with community businesses and organizations to create their projects. In most cases, adjustments will need to be made in order for educators to implement these lessons into their own courses.

Relationships are built through the networking process, and in some cases students have landed jobs with these organizations after graduation. It is important to tell students to contact organizations where they might like to work in the future and discuss potential project ideas. I close by providing examples of students who obtained jobs at the organizations where they'd done their school projects.

Chapter 5 is all about the nuts and bolts of tracking and assessing the project process. Project proposal forms, project progress forms, project completion forms, and personal reflection forms are used in my courses to help students stay on track. Progress forms are filled out numerous times so students can keep track of learning logs and artifacts they create and use in the process.

I mention in the chapter that these forms are not meant to be busywork but rather to provide instructors and students with tracking tools. These forms allow instructors to understand where students are at in the project process and encourage students to continue along the way to completion. Actual examples of these forms written by students are embedded in the chapter so readers can understand how they might use them for their own courses.

Chapter 6 provides real-world examples of project-based learning in colleges and schools. Interviews are offered from presidents and faculty of four different colleges that have individual programs—or, in some cases, entire colleges—using project-based learning. These administrators have taken a bold step and believe that project-based learning is a superior learning approach and therefore have encouraged multiple faculty at their schools to implement it.

I also interviewed school administrators who work for schools and school organizations implementing project-based learning throughout their entire curricula. These individuals are leading the way in education reform and changing the way teachers and administrators view education.

They all are using project-based learning, but some of them are implementing other innovative strategies as well, such as developing their own teacher education licensure programs and creating different administrative structures. These schools are changing how the world views education.

And finally, the conclusion summarizes all the book's key points, providing an overview of all the major points of project-based learning from theory to practice.

In the end, my goal for the book is to inspire readers to the point that they decide to implement the ideas contained herein.

Chapter One

Changing Education

Simon Sinek's book *Start with Why* offers a powerful and urgent message for the field of education. Although the book's primary audience is business leaders and focuses on how businesses and corporations should lead with a thorough understanding of their primary purpose, the education field should take notice and recapture its real purpose—inspiring students to continue learning throughout life, rather than training them to take tests.

Sinek (2009, 37) discusses the *golden circle*, which consists of three simple concepts: why, how, and what. The *why* is the most important of the three concepts. It is what inspires leaders to go to work every day and motivates them to attempt to accomplish what they truly are passionate about.

The real *why* for most educators probably centers on encouraging students to be curious and creative learners by building relationships with them and using effective teaching strategies that tap into their interests and passions. Unfortunately, the use of bubble tests in higher education and high school forces many educators to teach to the test.

The *hows* are the processes used to accomplish the company's goal of producing a certain number of products in a given time. Within a company, the processes are the structures and procedures used to build a better widget. The *hows* are the actions workers take in order to develop and build the products for their company. In education, the hows are the policies and procedures created to run a school or university, including the processes used in classrooms to help students learn.

The hows have taken over education. An enormous bureaucracy has been created centering on assessment procedures that prevent educators from their real purpose, which is inspiring students to learn. Data is driving our education systems, and students have become numbers rather than complex learning systems that all differ from one another.

The *whats* are the products created and built by a company's workers. They can also be routine tasks performed on a daily basis if the company is service-based. "Everyone is easily able to describe the products or services a company sells or the job function they have within that system. Whats are easy to identify" (Sinek 2009, 39).

In college and high school, the whats consists of the services provided by teachers, which means doling out information to students, and the products consists of the students' knowledge. Unfortunately, paper and pencil tests are the assessments used most often to determine this knowledge base.

Sinek argues that when corporate leaders build, promote, and market their company, they usually start with the what and then move to the how. They describe all the facts and details of the widget they want to build and attempt to convince consumers of its importance by describing what it is and what it can do. Then they move to the how and create or build processes to effectively and efficiently build the widget. The why is usually left out of this process altogether.

Apple Inc. is an example of a corporation that took a different approach and started with its why—which was to build something that would change peoples' lives. "Everything we do, we believe in changing the status quo. We believe in thinking differently. The way we challenge the status quo is by making our products beautifully designed, simple to use, and user friendly" (quoted in Sinek 2009, 41).

Early on when Apple began advertising, consumers did not even know what they were selling until the very end of the advertisement. The company wanted consumers to know that they too could think differently and change the status quo; they wanted them to have a kindred spirit with Apple. Apple was passionate about their product, and their passion and purpose drove their what and their how.

Unfortunately, education, like many companies, is focused on the what. It is focused on content, curriculum, and test scores; "people can understand vast amounts of complicated information, like facts and features, but it does not drive behavior" (Sinek 2009, 56). Administrators and educators can easily describe how a curriculum is used and test-score rankings because they are objective and demonstrable. Curricula and test-score rankings can be easily understood by administrators and parents without much difficulty, so education continues to focus on the what and not the why.

The real focus of education, however, should be trained on learning life skills, such as self-direction, problem solving, creativity, communication, collaboration, responsibility, and time management. But unfortunately, these skills have been replaced by memorizing information for tests. Today one rarely hears educators talk about their passion to turn students into inspired, motivated, lifelong learners. Instead, everything centers on improving test scores and assessment procedures. Education seems to have lost its real purpose.

The how is also more prevalent than the why in education. Educational bureaucracy continues to grow, and educational institutions incorporate new technologies in an attempt to streamline processes. Unfortunately, technology does not always make processes more effective and efficient.

Professors have chosen their careers because they are passionate about teaching, researching, and writing. But many universities continue to incorporate new technologies that prevent professors from engaging in their educational passions. In specific, program assessments, affirmative action, and the institutional-review boards (IRB) stand in the way.

UNIVERSITY BUREAUCRACY

Faculty members spend time creating assessment tools, inputting data into assessment software programs, and writing up program assessments. This, however, minimizes their time to pursue their real passions. One problem at certain universities is that there is a high turnover rate of assessment directors, and each time there is a new person in this position, a new software program is implemented.

Faculty members spend numerous hours trying to figure out how to use these software programs, which have mostly been clunky and counterintuitive. By the time instructors figure out how to use the assessment program, a new one is implemented.

Several years ago at a university in Southern Minnesota, one department spent a full day developing assessment tools and creating a portfolio process for its students, which they still use today but that they are no longer able to input into the new assessment software program. The department had created a wonderful assessment tool that included a portfolio, but it could no longer be used with the new assessment software program, so faculty members use it within their department but not within the university assessment system.

In addition, we might ask how much of this data is actually analyzed and used for any meaningful program improvements. How often do departments submit assessment reports never to receive any feedback for improvement? Spending this much time on the how prevents faculty from pursuing their why.

Perhaps because of liability issues affirmative-action offices have created search-committee processes that are excessive and cumbersome. Search committees are usually obligated to follow a set of predetermined steps that have been created by affirmative-action offices. In most cases, the search committee does all the work reviewing applications and interviewing candidates, but the dean often chooses whom to hire.

It is not uncommon today for search committees to undergo at least twenty steps in the hiring process, and at some universities faculty members must view a tutorial on these steps and then pass a quiz in order to serve on the committee. Faculty members are serving on search committees as a service to the university, yet are required to study for a quiz and pass it before they can serve. This lengthy step-by-step process is extremely time consuming and once again limits faculty from pursuing their purpose and passion.

The institutional review board process is also cumbersome, often requiring that applications be submitted via counterintuitive software programs. Proposal submission is usually a lengthy process that includes filling out applications, creating forms, and learning how to use the software program.

Faculty members at level-two research institutions typically teach three courses a semester, so they have limited time to conduct research. On top of having limited time, these faculty must spend a fair amount of time submitting an application through the IRB program in order to gain approval to conduct their research.

Many research projects that survey adults, however, are very low-risk and usually require that participants fill out online surveys or answer a very limited number of questions. In such cases, it seems that an IRB proposal is not even necessary, though it is still required if the data might be published.

If faculty had more time to pursue their purpose and passion, the university would be a better place for everyone. Students would enjoy their educational experience if they were around faculty who were excited and motivated about their own professional development, because this enthusiasm inevitably spills over into the classroom.

If time-consuming processes were eliminated or minimized, faculty would have more time to engage in their teaching and writing, creating a stimulating learning environment for students. Word of mouth about an enthusiastic professor, from one student to the next, is the best marketing tool possible.

Faculty want to be innovative and creative with their teaching and writing, but the hows keep getting in the way. According to the Higher Education Research Institute (n.d., 6), 74 percent of faculty surveyed across the United States in 2011 believed institutional procedures and red tape had significantly increased since the previous survey had been conducted in 1999.

The bureaucracy continues to grow, but must be trimmed and streamlined. I have been teaching at my university for fourteen years and have never felt so overwhelmed by the growing number of policies and procedures as I do today. Faculty energy is being drained by bureaucracy that prevents them from pursuing their why. The same thing is happening in public schools.

PUBLIC SCHOOL BUREAUCRACY

A number of reasons explain why individuals believe schools have a difficult time improving: underfunding, lack of technology, lack of sufficient student and parent involvement, the teaching model is broken compared to other countries, teacher unions prevent change, and the way performance is measured is flawed (Christenson, Horn, and Johnson 2008, 2–5). While these things are important to consider, there is another reason that overrides all others.

The stronghold from No Child Left Behind (NCLB) legislation and the Educational Testing Service continues to support a bureaucracy that spends billions of dollars on the production and use of standardized tests (Stiggins 2002). "In protest blogs, op-eds, and tweets, critics rail against 'billions and billions' spent on assessment, arguing that if only we stopped testing, then teachers' jobs, art classes, sports, school nurses, librarians, small classes, and more would be saved" (Tucker 2011, 22).

According to Butler (2014, 595) three educational reform efforts served as the basis for reauthorizing No Child Left Behind and the Race to the Top initiative: "All students are taught according to common instructional standards, students are tested throughout their academic career on their mastery of these standards, and educators and schools are held accountable for the results of students on these standards." Teachers must use the curricula they are given, help students practice for tests, proctor state-mandated tests during certain times of the year, and are held accountable for how well students do on these tests.

NCLB bureaucracy continues down a dead end, and these reform efforts prevent teachers from pursuing their passions. Essentially, teachers' hands are tied. Teachers have to stay abreast of curriculum changes, make sure they cover all the standards within a given time frame, and determine which tests to administer and when.

Most teachers probably did not enter the field of education in order to help students become better memorizers and test takers. They probably pursued this profession because they had an instructor who'd changed their life and inspired them to become an educator. Teachers become teachers because they believe in a purpose that goes beyond themselves—such as helping students become creative problem solvers and lifelong learners.

Unfortunately, teachers are not allowed to follow their real passion and purpose; instead, they are following the hows and whats of current legislation created by individuals who thought they knew what was best for students. As stated earlier, everyone within an organization can tell you *what* they do, and what teachers currently do is cover the curriculum standards and help students memorize information for standardized tests. Like in higher education, much of the K–12 focus is on the what and how, not the why.

Along a similar vein to Sinek's book is Pink's *Drive* (2009, 83–145), in which he identifies three crucial ingredients that motivate human beings: autonomy, mastery, and purpose. *Autonomy* is freedom to pursue and engage in personal passions and interests, *mastery* involves practicing skills and increasingly getting better at them, and *purpose* is believing that what one does matters to others and will have an impact beyond oneself.

Pink (2009, 9) argues that students in our public education system are not allowed to pursue autonomy, mastery, and purpose and instead have become focused on external rewards, which do not motivate them to learn: "Too many organizations—not just companies but governments and nonprofits as well—still operate from assumptions about human potential and individual performance that are outdated, unexamined, and rooted more in folklore than in science. They continue to pursue practices such as short-term incentive plans and pay-for-performance schemes in the face of mounting evidence that such measures usually don't work and often do harm. Worse, these practices have infiltrated our schools, where we ply our future workforce with iPads, cash, and pizza coupons to 'incentivize' them to learn."

When the primary goal of education is high test scores, then autonomy, mastery, and purpose are minimized. Students are being externally motivated to memorize information, and teachers are being externally motivated to have their students achive high test scores, which leads to job protection and more funding for the school. When high test scores are the goal of education, a variety of external motivators such as money and grades are used. The entire system is based on external motivators that in the long run harm students and teachers.

The education system promotes following step-by-step instruction down a path to a predetermined response or correct answer. This does not promote intrinsic motivation, critical thought, or creativity. Students graduate with the ability to follow directions, but are lost when placed in jobs that require the ability to be self-directed, creative, problem solvers.

Higher education and K–12 education systems need an adjustment, and at the very root of the problem is the learning process. Policymakers, administrators, educators, and parents must take a different view of the learning process in order for the system to change.

The primary learning process used to achieve high test scores is memorization, but as research suggests, students are apathetic and bored with this process. This is because they are not allowed to be autonomous, are not allowed to master skills important to them, and cannot see a purpose that goes beyond self. If the goal were to learn life skills, then the learning process would have to change.

Education would begin to change if teachers were allowed to pursue their passions and purpose, but it would change even more if students were allowed to do the same. In order for the field of education to change from a teacher-directed system to a more student-centered system, college and high school instructors must allow students to pursue their passions.

Learning ought not just be about memorizing information for tests. It ought to be about oneself and the skills needed to become a productive professional. Tapping into students' interests motivates them to learn, because the learning is relevant and meaningful. The stranglehold on testing and assessment procedures at both the college and high school levels must be broken so students can begin to learn on a deeper level.

COMPETENCY-BASED EDUCATION

There is a growing movement in higher education called *competency-based education* (CBE), which provides students with opportunities for deeper learning. CBE has been defined as "a combination of skills, abilities, and knowledge needed to perform a task in a specific context" (Jones and Voorhes 2002). According to Ordonez (2014, 48), "CBE models focus on experiential learning through real-world activities, giving students an alternative to the 'ivory tower' education of the past."

Competency-based education is based on acquiring the necessary competencies of a profession, which requires that students participate in real-world activities, also allowing them to use previous educational experiences for credit. Although originally created for adult learners returning to college after a hiatus, CBE is now being implemented for college students of all ages.

Prior learning assessment tools are being used by CBE schools and programs to determine the number of competencies that have already been acquired by students. Once prior competencies have been determined, students continue through their education, not taking seat-based courses but instead focusing on acquiring the remaining competencies.

I attended a CBE conference in March of 2015 and discovered that a number of colleges have CBE programs—including the University of Wisconsin–Madison, Purdue University, Lipscomb University, University of Michigan, DePaul University–School for New Learning, Western Governors University, Brandman University, Northern Arizona University, Alverno College, Excelsior College, Southern New Hampshire University, and Westminster College. Most of these programs incorporate designing and completing projects to demonstrate competency in specific skills associated with a particular profession.

Mintz (2015, 1) explains that competency-based learning incorporates projects to actively engage students. "To reinforce high levels of engagement, students do not simply view video-recorded lectures or review static websites; instead, they take part in active-learning activities and undertake career-aligned projects, including, where appropriate, fieldwork and clinical, laboratory, and research experiences."

Balcaen's (2013, 28) research focused on competency-based education and a critical thinking pedagogical framework. To explore this connection, he used several different design projects to determine students' level of engagement and found that this teaching approach was highly effective in helping students understand concepts on a deeper level. He also found that using the CBE model allowed students to practice critical thinking, an important life skill required in many professions.

Projects are the driving force behind many CBE programs because they not only allow students to demonstrate what they know but also allow instructors to assess their learning at the same time. CBE programs that incorporate designing and completing projects not only provide a flexible learning environment for students to master professional skills but also allow them to learn about themselves and how well they communicate, collaborate, and solve problems.

According to Johnstone and Soares (2014, 15–18), CBE has great potential to change the current higher education system into one that promotes "robust and valid competencies, allows students to learn at variable rates and [be] supported in their learning, allows students to access learning resources anytime, and provides assessments that are secure and reliable." With this type of education it is no longer about what students can remember for a test, it is about their demonstrating what they know by showing instructors what they can do.

Klein-Collins (2013, 5), senior director of research and policy development at the Council for Adult and Experiential Learning, believes that CBE has tremendous potential to change higher education on a broad scale. CBE, she says, "is increasingly in evidence outside of the adult learning bubble, with media coverage, congressional hearings, and an expansion—almost an explosion—of new program offerings across the country."

Soares (2012) believes that CBE has the potential to become a disruptive innovation and may eventually change higher education completely from a credit/course-based system to an experience-based system where students demonstrate and apply their knowledge in order to graduate from college. This disruption could dramatically change every aspect of higher education.

For example, credits would change to competencies, traditional seat-based courses would no longer exist, tuition would be based on competencies rather than credits, and instructors would no longer be paid based on the number of courses taught but, rather, on the number of students mentored through the CBE process. The entire system would have to be overhauled.

At the center of many CBE programs are projects which allow instructors to more easily assess competencies. For instance, when designing and completing a project, students create multiple artifacts such as "project reports, poster presentations/exhibition of the project, projects presentation, and log books for the project" (Petkov, Petkova, D'Onofrio, and Jarmoszko 2008, 242). In addition, students might create project proposals, weekly project-progress reports, and other forms of documentation of progress. These can all be used for assessment purposes. Lastly, the completed project itself is assessed as well.

These types of assessments are called *direct assessments* because students are observed when doing presentations and artifacts are products produced by the students that can easily be evaluated. Rubrics tend to be used most often when assessing projects, and Wiggins (1998, 168) suggests that there should be five criteria used when creating rubrics for project assessment: impact, craftsmanship, methods or processes used, content, and sophistication of performance. Educators can find numerous examples of rubrics online that have been used by high school and college instructors.

DEEPER LEARNING

According to Martinez and McGrath (2014, 3), a number of high schools around the country engage their students in deeper learning, which they define as a "process of preparing and empowering students to master essential academic content, think critically and solve complex problems, work collaboratively, communicate effectively, have an academic mindset, and be self-directed in their education."

Deeper learning focuses on the whole person and attempts to teach students life skills essential to solving daily problems, as well as how to become a productive professional able to collaborate with colleagues. High schools that adhere to the deeper learning philosophy implement six core strategies:

1. Create a cohesive, genuinely collaborative, school environment.
2. Make learning more active and engaging.
3. Integrate subjects with each other and with real-world issues.
4. Reach beyond school walls to make learning meaningful by involving partners in the wider community.
5. Inspire students by finding the "hooks" that motivate them.
6. Incorporate technology in ways that enrich and support learning experiences (Martinez and McGrath 2014, 21).

These are lofty strategies and might be difficult to implement in main-stream public schools. The individuals that Martinez and McGrath interviewed for their book were from eight different schools, several of which were charter schools. Charters are not obligated to follow all the regulations that traditional schools do, so this makes it easier for them to implement these six strategies.

There are reform organizations that believe in the principles of deeper learning and focus their efforts on school replication. EdVisions Inc., Big Picture Learning, Expeditionary Learning, High Tech High, New Tech High, and Envisions each receive funding to create schools. Most of these organizations started with one successful flagship school that allowed them to receive significant funding to replicate their schools.

For example, Envisions started its organization in 2002 and operates three small high-performing urban schools in the San Francisco Bay area. Its curriculum is based on the A–G Common Core coursework, which is intended to help students master the necessary skills to attend a four-year college. According to their website, educators in Envisions schools "create project-based assignments that challenge students to use the twenty-first-century skills of thinking critically, solving problems resourcefully, and collaborating productively that are needed to thrive in college, in future careers, and in life."

These organizations do not focus on helping students become better test takers; instead, they are helping them become better people by fostering life skills that will help them navigate their way through college and life in general. School replication is important to these organizations; however, what is more important is making sure that all their schools incorporate a significant amount of project-based learning, and use it as their primary teaching approach to foster academic and life skills development. This approach may be the reason why students in these schools are learning on a deeper level, because in-depth projects require them to become creative problem solvers, often working with peers to find solutions to school, community, and global problems.

Projects motivate students in these schools to learn because they are relevant and meaningful and because in most cases students are allowed to pursue projects based on their own interests and passions, which often results in their taking ownership of the learning process. Over time, project-based learning helps them become self-directed learners.

Can project-based learning help change education on a broader context and include traditional mainstream schools? The Hewlett Foundation seems to think so. It has created a network for deeper learning schools, and on their website they maintain that "a growing number of effective teachers, schools, and districts are proving that they can bring deeper learning to all students, from any background or neighborhood."

Lenz, Wells, and Kingston (2015, 15) echo this sentiment and believe that project-based learning, along with performance assessments, can help transform high school and college education in the United States. They argue that "project-based learning is the only realistic path to the deeper learning outcomes that this new century demands of us."

They believe that project-based learning can be implemented in all different types of schools, including mainstream public schools both big and small, charter schools, and private schools, regardless of state and federal policy, and that this teaching approach can transform education by allowing students to learn important life skills.

Project-based learning has the potential to transform education in both higher education and K–12, and the assessment process that accompanies it can help change education as well. This approach requires a different assessment system, because students demonstrate their learning to instructors and peers.

This is no different than what happens in the workplace, where employees engage in project work and are evaluated based on observable performance. Memorizing information for exams is not necessary with project-based learning because students *show* instructors what they know.

More and more educators are using project-based learning at all levels because when they use it they see how effective it is. They observe how it motivates students to learn and how it provides them with a variety of important benefits.

For example, Movahedzadeh, Patwell, Rieker, and Gonzalez (2012, 1) conducted a research study in which they turned an introductory molecular biology course into a project-based learning course to determine if students would enjoy it more and whether they would gain more knowledge about the topic, compared to in a traditional lecture/lab course. These researchers were extremely impressed with the outcomes of the course because it increased students' knowledge of complex biological issues, improved their self-confidence, motivated them to learn, and allowed them to incorporate critical thinking, collaboration, and problem-solving skills.

Many similar studies prove that project-based learning results in the development of a variety of life skills (Boss, Larmer, and Mergendoller, 2013). I have been using project-based learning and researching it for the past ten years and have also observed students developing important life skills as they create and complete a number of projects in an experiential education master's program.

In order for students to develop life skills, they must be given the freedom and autonomy to tap into their passions and interests. I feel fortunate that I teach at the graduate level because most of the students enter the program with a fair amount of life experience and are self-motivated to learn and complete their studies. However, undergraduates and high school students I have worked with were also extremely excited and engaged in their learning after tapping into their interests.

Educators should tell students to think about their interests and prompt them with questions, such as: What are you most excited about doing in your career? What do you want to change in your community or on a global level? What would you like to be known for by your colleagues and peers? Breaking students into small groups to discuss these types of questions allows them the opportunity to create a project that taps into their passion.

Being passionate about a project is critical, because students tend to persevere through the process of completing it. And when they persevere, they learn crucial life skills such as problem solving, creativity, communication, collaboration, time management, responsibility, and work ethic.

Project-based learning is helping change education as more and more high school and college educators use it every day. Research on this topic continues to grow and is proving that project-based learning enhances life skills development.

Educators in the trenches realize that standardized tests do not motivate students to learn; these teachers understand the importance of involving students in the learning process. Project-based learning taps into the students' interest and motivates them to pursue learning that is meaningful and relevant. The time has come to focus on helping students develop important life skills that they can use long after they graduate from school.

Chapter Two

Project-Based Learning
and Skill Development

Project-based learning has been defined as "a teaching method where teachers guide students through a problem-solving process [that] includes identifying a problem, developing a plan, testing the plan against reality, and reflecting on the plan while in the process of designing and completing a project" (Wurdinger et al. 2007, 151). This definition places emphasis on a student-centered approach to learning. With this approach, students design and complete projects, many of which require solving multiple problems during the process.

Solving problems in order to complete a project takes more time than passive methods of learning, because students will have to undergo multiple trial-and-error attempts before completing the project to their satisfaction. This is an important concept for educators to understand before attempting to implement project-based learning (PBL) in their classrooms.

With this teaching approach, students create and produce projects. For instance, students might construct a model from a blueprint, design a Web page, or create a learning portfolio as a project. Some educators are more teacher-directed with this approach and identify the projects for students, whereas others are more student-centered, allowing students to create their own projects based on their own interests.

Schools are often the determining factor as to whether the educator can be student-centered or teacher-directed. In traditional public school settings, teachers may have to be more teacher-directed because of time constraints. If educators only have fifty-minute class periods, then they may have to use a teacher-directed approach and identify the projects for the students, whereas charter schools, especially those with a project-based emphasis, can be more student-centered, allowing students to create their own projects.

At the college level, class size may be the determining factor as to whether instructors are more student-centered or teacher-directed. In smaller classes, instructors may be able to implement project-based learning more easily and are likely able to provide more individual attention to each student, which allows for a student-centered approach. In larger classes, it may be more difficult to guide all the students through the project-based learning process, so identifying the projects for students may be more manageable.

HISTORICAL ROOTS OF PROJECT-BASED LEARNING

Project-based learning is not a new concept; it has been around since the mid-1800s. Knoll (1997) wrote an interesting piece on the history of project-based learning that explains in great detail how it evolved and changed from both European and US influences.

He discovered through his research that the project method was being used by the Massachusetts Institute of Technology's engineering faculty as early as 1864. The teaching method gained support from school administrators and teachers during this time period, and by 1897 it was being used with "thousands of males and females at American high schools" in carpentry, ironwork, cooking, and sewing courses (Knoll 1997, 4). Some of the early polytechnic universities in the United States placed tremendous importance on projects and often required students to complete a major project in order to graduate.

Project-based learning almost lost its foothold just as it was gaining momentum in the early 1900s. William Kilpatrick, a student of John Dewey's, and one of the early leaders of the progressive education movement, created confusion about project-based learning by suggesting that a project could be anything as long as it was initiated by the student.

In his essay "The Project Method," Kilpatrick (1918) suggested that students did not need to be actively involved in the project and could sit passively listening to music, for example, in order to complete a project. Kilpatrick's essay was based on John Dewey's (1913) *Interest and Effort in Education*, and, according to Knoll (1997), Dewey disagreed with Kilpatrick's interpretation.

Dewey believed that teachers are critical to the educational process and should guide students through experiences to enhance learning outcomes. Although Dewey agreed with much of Kilpatrick's essay, he argued that teachers ought to be involved in guiding the student through the project process.

Later, Kilpatrick recanted and agreed that the educational process should not be left to the sole responsibility of the student. The disagreement had been settled, and the project method continued gaining attention both in K–12 and higher education settings.

Stillman Robinson, professor of mechanical engineering at Illinois Industrial University, Dewey and Kilpatrick's contemporary, had the correct conception of project-based learning, because he required his students to not only draw blueprints of machines but also create working products off their blueprints (Knoll 1997). He believed that projects should be created and built by students so that they could understand their practical importance. Project-based learning has come a long way since Kilpatrick, Dewey, and Robinson's time and continues to be used by schools and educators all across the world today.

WHY USE PROJECT-BASED LEARNING?

In his book *Creating Innovators*, Wagner (2012) writes of how he interviewed college students, parents, teachers, and employers in an attempt to discover key elements that help individuals become innovative thinkers. One of the key themes that recurs throughout these interviews is the use of projects in the learning process.

After interviewing several students whom he considered innovative thinkers, Wagner concluded, "Once again, we see the importance of an outlier teacher whose collaborative, project-based, interdisciplinary approach to learning had a profound effect on the development of a young person" (2012, 78–79). This process of learning promotes creative thinkers and motivates students to learn. It works and should be used by educators at all levels in education.

Multiple research studies suggest that when students are engaged in creating and completing projects they learn important life skills such as problem solving, time management, responsibility, and collaboration (Blumenfeld, Soloway, Marx, Krajcik, Guzdial, and Palincsar 1991; Grant and Branch 2005; Levine 2002; Littky and Grabelle 2004; Newell 2003; Thomas, Enloe, and Newell 2005). Increasingly, K–12 teachers and college instructors around the world are beginning to use this method because they know it challenges students on an individual level, motivating and inspiring them by tapping into their own learning styles (Bender 2012).

Proof That It Works in Higher Education

Multiple research studies in higher education suggest that students are engaged in their learning when creating and completing projects and that they

learn important life skills such as problem solving, time management, responsibility, and collaboration (Hall, Palmer, and Bennett 2012; Starobin et al.
2014; Wolff 2003; Zhang, Peng, and Hung 2009). Krauss and Boss (2013,
18) also identified important life skills that students learn while engaged in
PBL, which included flexibility, organization, self-control, task initiation,
time management, and metacognition.

Other researchers have analyzed different benefits of using project-based
learning such as student achievement, creativity, motivation, and teamwork.
Barak and Dori (2005, 117), for example, conducted a research study with
college freshman chemistry students and discovered that the project-based
experimental group outperformed the control group, the members of which
were exposed to traditional textbook chemistry problems. After being involved in a project requiring the construction of molecular models, the
project-based group scored higher on their final exams and "enhanced their
understanding of chemical concepts, theories, and molecular structures."

Zhou (2012) conducted a qualitative research study with twenty first-year
engineering students who were enrolled in a project-based learning course.
He discovered that students believed creativity was extremely important in
helping them to design projects, to become more effective team members,
and to improve motivation to learn.

Palmer and Hall (2011, 363) also conducted a study with engineering
students, asking them questions about their experience with project courses.
They sent out 237 surveys and received 72 back. They categorized some of
their findings as "best aspects" and found that students enjoyed working in
teams, believed that real-world applications were important, would rather
do project work than take examinations, enjoyed exposure to professional
engineering work, and thought the instructors were helpful and supportive.

Jollands, Jolly, and Molyneaux (2012, 152) interviewed twenty graduates
from a school of civil, chemical, and environmental engineering. Some of
these students had been enrolled in several project courses, and others had
not. Both groups recognized that enrolling in project courses resulted in
benefits such as project management skills, time management, confidence,
communication skills, and systems thinking.

I conducted a study with a doctoral student in which graduate students
were surveyed and interviewed before and after taking a semester-long course
using project-based learning. The course consisted of reading and discussing
several books, discussing the structure and format for projects, completing
one in-depth project, and presenting the project at the end of the course.

The survey consisted of thirty-five questions, each attached to one of eight
life skills. For instance, questions two, four, fifteen, twenty-one, and thirty-
one were associated with problem solving. The same pre- and postsurveys

were given to students to determine if there was any growth in life skills development after taking the sixteen-week course. Interestingly, we found that five of the eight life skills had a statistically significant increase from the before- and after-course surveys (Wurdinger and Qureshi 2014, 4). In this study, several students were interviewed, and the themes identified all focused on enhancing their life skills development. Figure 2.1 shows the average scores before and after the course was taken.

I use project-based learning in all of my courses, which are at the graduate level, and students appreciate the freedom to create and develop projects that are meaningful and relevant to their careers. At the end of one of my courses, I asked the students to write down what they had learned most from doing their projects.

Interestingly, their responses focused more on life skills development than on specific academic content. For example, they mentioned skills like problem solving, taking initiative, and time management. They were learning useful skills that they could transfer to other learning situations and to future employment opportunities.

Project-based learning engages students in their learning at all levels. Imagine if college and high school students could work on projects in all their classes and ask as many questions as they liked while practicing skills such as problem solving, critical thinking, time management, and responsibility.

According to Pearlman (2006), in order to compete in the future, students need a different set of skills than most are currently learning—including

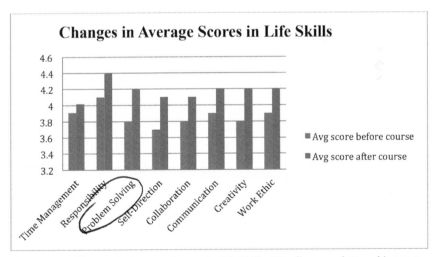

Figure 2.1. Changes in Average Scores in Life Skills (Wurdinger and Qureshi, 2014)

learning and thinking skills, technology literacy skills, and life skills—and these skills can best be obtained through project-based learning. Educators should give students opportunities to participate in project-based learning so they can practice these skills.

Although project-based learning is a more intensive learning process than memorizing information, it does require more time to implement but allows for deeper learning, which inspires and motivates students. The learning is rich.

Students learn useful skills that they carry with them after they graduate, which has a lasting effect on their lives. Project-based learning not only allows students to be actively involved in the learning process, it also allows them to learn important life skills.

These research studies suggest that PBL is effective with multiple age levels because it taps into students' interests and allows them to create projects that result in meaningful learning experiences. It is one approach to teaching that inspires students to learn and provides them with relevant problems to solve (Blumenfeld et al. 1991; Grant and Branch 2005; Levine 2002; Littky and Grabelle 2004; Thomas, Enloe, and Newell 2005; Newell 2003).

At the K–12 level, charter and private schools have fewer restrictions from federal education policies and are able to design their own curricula, so they are able to integrate project-based learning more than mainstream public schools. Jason Ravitz, research and evaluation consultant and former director of research at the Buck Institute for Education, estimates teachers in approximately five thousand schools in the United States have been recipients of project-based materials and/or have been provided workshops on this topic (personal communication, September 2013). So, PBL is gaining ground, but not fast enough.

In higher education, one is likely to find individual faculty members using project-based learning. However, several undergraduate programs at Olin College and several undergraduate and graduate programs at MIT are using it extensively (Wagner 2012).

Neumont University in South Jordan, Utah, and Westminster College in Salt Lake City integrate project-based learning in many of their courses. At Worcester Polytechnic Institute, students complete a major qualifying project in the students' major fields of study that allows them to spend a significant amount of time on an in-depth project.

Organizations such as the Buck Institute for Education and Edutopia provide numerous resources that help educators integrate project-based learning into their curriculums. Their primary focus is on how to integrate it into K–12 schools that are bound to the traditional structures, such as compartmentalized subject matter, shorter class periods, and student achievement based on test scores. While this is definitely a step in the right direction, these structures often promote a teacher-directed approach in which the teacher determines what projects students will complete, which does not necessarily promote student motivation or interest.

K–12 Research

Researchers have analyzed teacher acceptance, student motivation, and student achievement, and all have come to the conclusion that PBL is an effective teaching methodology. Barron et al. (1998) discovered that academic performance and motivation are greatly improved when using project-based learning.

In their comprehensive study, they had students create blueprints of chairs and playhouses and then present these drawings to their classmates. They measured low, average, and high achieving students and found that all three groups had significant improvements in their ability to understand difficult math concepts after using the project method.

This approach to learning not only had a significant impact on their comprehension, but it also had a positive impact on their motivation. Fifty percent of the students interviewed about their experience specifically mentioned that the projects were a very important part of their school year (Barron et al. 1998, 305).

Cornell and Clarke (1998) conducted an extensive study on standards-based teaching and learning for the primary purpose of moving teachers away from a teacher-directed lecture format toward a student-centered format where students initiated and completed projects. The authors found that students were more engaged when involved in project-based learning because it gave them an opportunity to work with other students while doing hands-on activities, which provided them with a more self-directed learning environment. Even lower performing students enjoyed the process because it not only gave them an opportunity to discover unique skills necessary to completing projects but also allowed them to progress at their own pace.

However, Cornell and Clarke (1998, 94) discovered paradoxically that "less teacher talk requires more teacher time" and "free-ranging self-directed inquiry depends on a tight design structure," indicating that, even though motivation and student learning were enhanced through the project-based learning process, the methodology requires more work for teachers when designing projects and preparing lessons. Teachers commented that the initial phase of the project-based learning process required a fair amount of planning time; however, once that had been established, teachers were able to focus more on guiding students through the process.

Liu and Hsiao (2002, 311) conducted a research study on using project-based learning with middle school students and found that it increased their "learning of design knowledge, their cognitive-strategy use, and their motivation toward learning." In this study, students assumed the roles of researcher, graphic artist, programmer, project manager, and audio/visual specialist and worked together to complete multimedia presentations.

Because students were directly involved in the process, they were able to understand and retain the information they were using while creating and designing their multimedia presentation. Their research clearly indicates that project-based learning has the potential to enhance both student motivation and performance in the classroom. Liu and Hsiao (2002, 303) sum up their research by claiming that students showed "substantial gains in their abilities to understand, use, and present geometric concepts."

I conducted a yearlong study with several colleagues at a local middle school looking at teacher acceptance and student engagement, and we discovered that providing a one-day staff training to educate teachers on how to use project-based learning enhances and promotes teacher acceptance, which is critical to implementing and sustaining the use of this method in school settings (Wurdinger et al. 2007, 158).

Some teachers in this study used individual projects, and others used group projects, but in either situation teachers supported the use of this method because they observed a high level of motivation when students were engaged with their projects. Some teachers stated that students were so engrossed with their projects that they did not notice the teacher was in the room.

As noted by Fullan (2001, 115), "Educational change depends on what teachers do and think—it's as simple and as complex as that." Without teacher acceptance, innovative methods like project-based learning won't make it through the door of the classroom.

In another study, I sent out online surveys to the alumni, students, teachers, and parents of the student-centered, project-based learning charter school Minnesota New Country School in Henderson, Minnesota, in order to explore definitions of success and determine how well this school teaches life skills. One hundred and forty-seven surveys were collected from these four groups.

Students and alumni ranked themselves extremely high in their life skills. Table 2.1 depicts the percentages of combined good and excellent responses on how alumni and students ranked themselves in life skills.

In comparison, alumni and students ranked themselves much lower in academic skills such as study skills, note-taking, and test-taking. Even though alumni ranked themselves low in academic skills, 50 percent of those polled

Table 2.1. **Percentages of Combined Good and Excellent Responses**

Life Skills	Alumni	Students
Creativity	100	91
Problem solving	95	84
Time management	87	66
Finding information	100	84
Learning how to learn	91	82
Self-direction	92	76

graduated from college, which is considerably higher than the national average of 39 percent (Wurdinger and Rudolph 2009, 122).

In another study, a colleague and I surveyed students from a project-based-learning charter school in Saint Paul, Minnesota, called Avalon. The survey asked several open-ended questions about the students' experience at Avalon; here are several of their responses:

Project-based learning helped my focus in college as well as my ability to communicate with others. Avalon gave me excellent writing, listening, reading comprehension and time management skills.

[Avalon had] a semi-structured system rather than just assignments to be done; it gave me an edge in creative thinking. Avalon [is] overall very similar to college, which is not what I hear from other students.

Avalon increased my ability to pursue things I want to learn (unlike many students) plus advantages in making strong, well thought out presentations.

[Avalon] taught me to reach my goals, hard work, creativity, risk-taking and never being afraid to ask for help.

Avalon taught me to work on my own; create what I want to do in life.

Avalon gave me advantages in life by igniting my passion for learning so even when I'm not in school I am continually searching for ways to better my life and keep myself an active member of community.

Avalon helped teach me the value of community; Avalon taught me to find my goals and dreams and run after them.

I see learning and school as an enjoyable challenge and am more motivated to continue school than some peers.

Self-reliance and independence allow me to direct my life where [I] want to go
with less outside support. (Wurdinger and Enloe 2011, 90–91)

It is obvious from reading these statements that Avalon students enjoyed their
school experience and that they learned important life skills while attending.
Avalon and Minnesota New Country School are unique in that projects drive
the curriculum and state standards are met through completing projects.

The role of the instructor at these schools is to help guide students through
their projects, and therefore this process requires instructors to develop
strong relationships with students. These schools are smaller, and students
are placed in advisories that consist of typically around fifteen students per
advisor. This is a luxury that allows teachers to spend more one-on-one time
with students, and this might be the reason why students develop strong life
skills while attending these schools.

In the May/June 2011 issue of *American Teacher*, the article "Project
Learning Links School with After School" discusses linking school with after-school activities. The article states that after-school project-based learning
opportunities should "differ from regular school because projects can suffer
when time must be tightly controlled; provide opportunities to tap students'
interests; engage children in working collaboratively; provide a real-world
context in which to apply academic content; move students towards a goal; let
them relax, unwind, and be less formal; build success and pride; help kids see
the practical uses for whatever they are studying; and provide more choices
than students get during the regular school day" (American Federation of
Teachers 2011, 4). The article suggests this is something that should occur
after school as extracurricular activities. But if PBL actually does all these
things, then why shouldn't it be used in the regular curriculum?

A fair amount of research was covered in both higher education and K–12
settings because educational administrators often ask for research that sup-
ports the implementation of a new learning strategy. They want proof that it
works in order to determine whether they want to spend money to implement
it in their schools and colleges.

EXPERIENTIAL LEARNING AND PROJECT-BASED LEARNING

In 2009, a colleague and I wrote *Teaching for Experiential Learning*, which
discusses a variety of teaching approaches that promote hands-on learning.
These approaches, which include active/collaborative learning, problem/
inquiry-based learning, service learning, place-based learning, and project-
based learning, are all based on certain principles including "promoting
hands-on learning, using a problem-solving process, addressing real-world

problems, encouraging student interaction with each other and the content, engaging in direct experiences, and using multiple subjects to enhance inter-disciplinary learning" (Wurdinger and Carlson 2009, 8). With this process, students are actively pursuing their learning, are provided more freedom to explore and discover knowledge, and may collaborate in seeking answers to problems.

The underlying theme with all these approaches is helping students be-come active participants in the learning process; however, each approach has its own subtle nuances that makes it unique from the others. Place-based learning, for example, often includes some aspect of environmental educa-tion and focuses on learning about the place or community where one lives. Service learning, on the other hand, is about providing some type of service to the community that offers students an opportunity to learn how to be more civically engaged and take responsibility for helping a community become a better place to live in.

They are all unique. However, many articles and books on these different approaches tend to use the term *projects* to describe the learning process. In referring to place-based learning, Sobel (2005, 19) states that "place-based educators want to advocate for an integrated curriculum that emphasizes project-based learning, teacher collaboration, and extensive use of commu-nity resources and volunteers," and in his book on problem-based learning, Barrel (2007, 11) states that "during a reflective session on a long-range inquiry project I asked several teachers what they had learned about inquiry."

In addition, when discussing these different experiential approaches, col-leagues and students often refer to their service learning projects, place-based learning projects, and problem-based projects. A project denotes a product that is created to have useful applications. For example, making a fishing lure or a piece of jewelry requires that one plan what the lure or jewelry will look like and test out the ideas by actually making prototypes. In the end, the project is useful because you can wear jewelry or catch a fish with a lure.

The word *project* is used in connection with these experiential approaches to learning and is a common denominator of all of them. These approaches all use projects to explain their theories and practices, and therefore the term *project-based learning* may be a more universal and accurate term than the other experiential approaches mentioned.

There are also potential problems with these experiential approaches to learning. For example, active/collaborative learning and problem/inquiry-based learning may be steeped in theory and lacking in practice if students are allowed to discuss their ideas in the classroom about how to solve a problem but are not allowed to test these ideas against reality to determine whether they work or not.

Similarly, if students fill grocery bags with food at a food shelf for a service learning activity or till ground for a community garden for a place-based learning activity, they are not engaged in problem solving and instead may see it as mere manual labor. In such cases, the activities are heavy on practice but light on theory. Students are doing hands-on activities, yes, but if they are not doing any problem solving—or don't see the bigger picture behind why they are doing these activities—then the theoretical connections are lacking.

Project-based learning can help eliminate this problem by balancing theory with practice. When projects are integrated into all of these approaches, students must create plans, test them out, and reflect on the outcome. After using all these approaches in my classes, I have come to the conclusion that project-based learning should be incorporated into all of these approaches.

Figure 2.2 depicts five common experiential approaches to learning that show how one approach incorporates the one before it when moving from the inside to the outside rings. Project-based learning, depicted in the triangle, shows that it is possible to incorporate it into all of the other approaches to varying degrees.

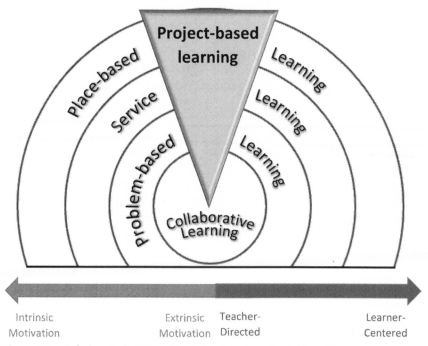

Figure 2.2.   Infusing Project-Based Learning into Experiential Learning

Project-based learning may be incorporated with collaborative learning and problem-based learning; however, it is used more heavily with service-based learning and place-based learning. The approaches in the outer rings tend to be more student-centered and are therefore more intrinsically motivating, whereas collaborative and problem-based learning tend to be more teacher-directed and are more extrinsically motivating.

The two approaches on the inside rings are easier to implement in classroom settings and therefore tend to be used more often in traditional classrooms. The approaches in the outside rings tend to be more time consuming to implement and often require students to move outside the classroom into the community to complete projects.

Students can create plans for a project, but the learning becomes experiential when they begin to build it with their hands and then test it out to see if it works. Problem solving tends to be one of the fundamental life skills that students learn as a by-product of the project-based learning process.

The reason for this is because in-depth projects require solving multiple problems that crop up during the process of completing a project. The learning theory that occurs with project-based learning stems from Dewey's (1938b, 101–19) "pattern of inquiry." Dewey's pattern of inquiry consists of six steps. His explanation of this theory, however, is very similar to the scientific method.

Dewey explained that a relevant problem causes perplexity and desire to find an answer (step one), which is then followed by creating a plan (step two), testing the plan against reality (step three), and reflecting on its worth (step four). The planning and testing phases of this process are what make learning experiential. Responding to instructor questions and reciting back information in traditional classroom settings allows students to talk, but learning becomes experiential when they create plans to solve problems and test them in real-world scenarios.

For example, conducting a restoration project for a local hiking trail entails creating a plan to determine what parts of the trail need to be restored, where the trail might be eroding, what type of material will be needed to restore the trail, how to transport the material to the trail locations, determining what tools will be needed to transport and move materials, and figuring out the number of people needed to do the work. Questions and problems will crop up during the process of completing the project, which might require several trial-and-error attempts during each phase of the process before the project is completed.

When students are in the process of completing a project, they go through the process of identifying problems, developing plans, testing them against reality, and reflecting on them to determine their worth. This process challenges

Project-Based Learning Process

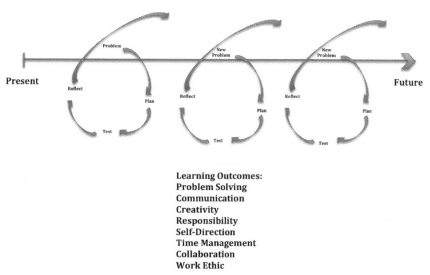

Learning Outcomes:
Problem Solving
Communication
Creativity
Responsibility
Self-Direction
Time Management
Collaboration
Work Ethic

Figure 2.3.   Learning Outcomes of the Project-Based Learning Process

students cognitively as they attempt to construct the project and solve problems they encounter in the process of completing it.

Projects are typically complex and entail going through multiple trial-and-error attempts before the project is completed. Each time students go through this cycle (problem, plan, test, reflect) they solve problems and learn from their mistakes.

Figure 2.3 shows how the project-based learning process begins in the present and leads students out into the future as they work through multiple problem-solving episodes. They become discoverers of knowledge, and each cycle requires that they practice and learn skills such as problem solving, creativity, time management, responsibility, work ethic, and self-direction. The skills they learn from going through this process are critical.

COLLATERAL LEARNING

In 1938 John Dewey wrote an influential book, *Experience and Education*, in which he discusses the importance of collateral learning: "Collateral learning in the way of formation of enduring attitudes, of likes and dislikes, may be and often is much more important than the spelling lesson or lesson in geography or history that is learned. For these attitudes are fundamentally what count in the future. The most important attitude that can be formed is that of desire to go on learning" (Dewey 1938a, 49). This is what happens with project-based learning. In learning environments where students are given freedom to determine their own projects based on their interests, as well as freedom to work on projects at their own pace, they begin to learn how to learn and learn how to be self-directed learners. They are working on completing a project but as a result are learning other skills as by-products of the process.

Oftentimes students are unaware that they are learning these skills. During focus-group sessions with students from Minnesota New Country School, a project-based charter school in south-central Minnesota, the students were asked what they were learning by doing their projects. At first they began talking about content standards they were learning, because these are required by the state and are at the forefront of each project.

But when asked what specific types of skills that they could apply from one project to another, they began to mention things like problem solving, responsibility, time management, flexibility, and initiative. Once one person mentioned one or two of these life skills, the others began to chime in, and the list began to grow.

Students are using their hands to make the project and are engaged because the project has significance to them. Engagement, motivation, hands-on learning, and problem solving are collateral skills that students learn, and they often learn them simultaneously while in the process of completing projects.

THINGS TO CONSIDER WHEN
IMPLEMENTING PROJECT-BASED LEARNING

Both of my daughters attended traditional mainstream schools, but both of them had several innovative teachers that used project-based learning with great success. Project examples that their teachers assigned included creating life collages, designing Web pages for the school, producing television commercials, and building small wooden boats. As a parent it was interesting to observe their behavior when they were involved in project work as opposed to when they were doing traditional homework consisting mostly of reading textbooks and filling out worksheets.

Both of my daughters were highly motivated and excited, whether working in groups or alone to create their projects. No prompting was necessary to work on their projects after school. They would come home from school, immediately clear off the dining room table, and spread out all of their project materials.

flow

As they worked on their projects, they would lose track of time, creating what was in their minds masterpieces. They were so immersed in the process that we would have to force them to stop and clear the table so we could eat dinner.

Some educators give students the freedom to determine what they want to create for a project and provide guidance through the project process only when necessary. In other cases, educators provide students with predetermined projects and control the process from beginning to end. The topics were chosen for my daughters, but the teachers provided students with the freedom to determine what they could include in their projects.

Project-based learning is the centerpiece of the curriculum for some college and high school programs, and with others it is used sparingly as extracurricular activities. In the former, students do all projects to complete their graduation requirements, whereas in the latter they might be used as afterschool activities to promote social skills.

Projects may be highly structured, requiring detailed project proposals, learning outcomes, and exhibitions that are evaluated with performance-based rubrics, or they may be unstructured, nongraded activities (how to track the project process is discussed in detail in chapter 5). The type of project-based learning that will be discussed here is intentionally designed by the instructor to be part of the curriculum. However, educators can easily modify these ideas into nongraded extracurricular activities.

What Variation to Use

Newell (2007) created five variations of project-based learning that explain how it is used in classroom settings. The variations are like a spectrum, with number one being entirely teacher-directed and number five being student-directed. Teachers control the entire process on one end and students on the other. It may be helpful for educators to determine what variation they wish to utilize and use the corresponding guidelines as a tool to help implement project-based learning with their students:

1. Project is teacher-controlled
   Project is part of curricular unit, text, etc.
   All students do the same thing
   No student choice
   Graded as part of class unit
2. Project is teacher-controlled
   Allows for student inquiry, choice of topic within curriculum
   Students have to frame their own questions

All students have same time frame
Graded as part of class unit

3. Project is set up and orchestrated by teacher
   Project is inquiry-based, looks at "big picture," still curriculum-based
   Project is interdisciplinary and thematic in nature
   Students may be in cooperative groups, teaming
   Performance, product assessment is used as well as class grade

4. Project is created with teacher-student interaction
   Project is interdisciplinary in nature, inquiry-based, authentic
   Rubrics assess performances, critical thinking, and problem solving
   Students may be in cooperative groups, teaming, or whole class
   Includes place-based, community service, etc.
   Time frame is negotiable but within semester or units

5. Project is student-driven, authentic
   Project is teacher-facilitated, with teachers providing the process
   The "whole world" is the curriculum, with state standards guiding the work
   Rubrics assess learning-to-learn skills, individual development, etc.
   Performance and products assessed, performances to real-world audience
   May be individual or group projects
   Could include place-based community service projects
   Nongraded, time frame is negotiable

Variation five is highly student-directed and requires more freedom and larger blocks of time to implement, which may be impractical for educators in more traditional, mainstream education settings. Variations one and two might be more practical for educators who are new to project-based learning, which will allow them to experiment using more control over the process and provide an easier transition to the other variations as they progress toward a more student-centered classroom.

Even though variations one and two limit students' freedom in choosing their own projects, the methods still enhance student motivation and therefore can be extremely effective. Newell (2003) argues, however, that variations four and five are more effective because when students choose projects of their own passion they have a vested interest in pursuing and completing them. Unfortunately, few teachers in traditional, mainstream settings have the luxury of allowing their students to choose projects of their own interest.

Working Alone or in Groups

After deciding which variation is most appropriate for your classroom setting, you will want to determine whether students will work alone or if they will be allowed to work together on their projects. This will require some thinking and planning on the instructor's part because there are definite advantages and disadvantages to each.

For instance, a disadvantage of students working alone means the student will be doing all of his or her own work, which will require a longer period of time to complete the project than if working in a group. However, the disadvantage of working in a group might result in one or two students doing most if not all of the work.

If you choose to allow students to work together, then you may want to create some guidelines for the process. Identifying specific tasks for each student will help spread the workload more evenly. You might also want to identify specific jobs within the group, such as information collectors, interviewers, recorders, time keepers, builders, designers, and others, so that everyone understands their roles and expectations within the group.

If projects require larger amounts of time to complete, you may need to provide groups with benchmarks throughout the semester so they are more apt to follow this time line and complete the project when it is due. Reporting on their progress periodically will also help them stay on track and allows them an opportunity to discuss problems they have encountered along the way.

From my own personal experience, group work is more challenging to manage; however, participating students learn communication and trust-building skills that they otherwise wouldn't if they were working alone. Graduate students in my classes often seem to prefer working alone because they can create and design projects fashioned around their own personal interests. Otherwise, they may compromise their own interests and end up working on someone else's project with little or no motivation.

Educators new to this approach might consider having their students work alone when trying to implement this approach for the first time because it is easier to manage and assess learning outcomes. Group work can be used once the educator becomes more familiar with the project-based process.

There is a tremendous amount of information on theories and practices of designing and implementing group work, which is beyond the scope of this book. For more detailed information about creating effective group work, three books come to mind: *Designing Group Work* by Elizabeth Cohen and Rachel Lotan (2014), *Communicating in Small Groups* by Beebe and Masterson (2014), and *Effective Groups* by Cannon and Guthrie (2006).

Classroom Culture

After determining whether students will work alone, in groups, or in a combination of the two, you will need to implement a different classroom culture and relinquish some control. No doubt educators need to help students identify manageable projects, but they also need to allow their classes to muddle their way through the process. Projects should be intellectually challenging so that students engage in critical thinking during the planning, testing, and reflecting phases, but not too challenging; otherwise students may get discouraged, which could bring the learning process to a sudden halt.

If an educator retains too much control, however, the learning process may be hindered. For example, when an educator provides students with a handout explaining a step-by-step process on how to construct a project and then demonstrates step by step how to do it, little if any problem solving will occur. The students are not challenged in this situation because they simply replicate what the educator tells them to do.

Problem solving will become an integral part of the learning process if this same educator explains to students that they need to build something with certain materials and resources and then allows them to experiment and build it on their own. Challenging students by providing them with opportunities for creative thought allows them to explore and determine what the best design and building process might be, and this requires letting go of some control.

Using project-based learning is challenging but rewarding, especially when students become motivated, self-directed learners. With this approach, educators take a less visible role in the classroom, guiding students through the learning process by encouraging them to take risks and challenging them to learn from their mistakes, because that is how humans learn. Students are given more freedom to explore the learning process, and the educator's role is to help them when they get stuck so they can keep moving forward with their learning. Educators are not the center of attention in the classroom; student learning is.

A different type of classroom culture needs to be created when using this teaching approach. The role of the educator is a facilitator or guide with the purpose founded in guiding students in designing meaningful projects and allowing them time to complete and demonstrate their comprehension to an audience of peers.

Students become active participants with this teaching approach and need to understand that a different culture combined with a set of expectations is a beneficial way to learn. Changing the classroom culture requires a change in the educator's role and the student's role, as well as a change in the classroom structure.

With this approach, students should not be confined to their chairs. Students need to experience their learning in a less directed way to fully benefit from this teaching approach. To engage in their learning, students need autonomy, which may include brainstorming ideas with peers, moving around the classroom, school buildings, or campus to gather resources and use technology to access information.

The project-based classroom may appear chaotic; however, freedom, along with clear expectations, allows students to move around to get the information needed to continue moving forward in the process. It appears chaotic to a casual observer because students are moving around; but when it is conducted properly, students are focused on what they need to do to move forward in the learning process.

With this approach, educators can have as large or as small of a role during the active phase of learning. For example, in a science class students could be given the project of implementing ten environmental practices to conserve more energy and provide a presentation to the class on these practices. The educators could provide students with a variety of different practices and then allow students the freedom to choose and implement these different practices on their own, or they could tell students they have to find these practices on their own.

The most important underlying theme is that through this approach students will become engaged in learning and begin to learn important life skills. Providing opportunities that allow for creativity, direct experience, and personal interpretation will not only engage students in their learning but will also perhaps promote a more humanistic approach to education. Below are a few ideas educators might want to discuss with students before using these methods.

Educator's Role

1. The educator will act as a guide, allowing students to make mistakes and learn from them along the way.
2. The educator will provide students with freedom to experiment in order to discover solutions to the problems they encounter.
3. The educator will provide students with resources and information when they get stuck so that they can continue moving forward with their learning.

Students' Role

1. Students will be allowed freedom to move around the classroom or campus as long as they are moving forward in the learning process.
2. Students will need to understand that making mistakes and failing is part of the learning process.
3. Students should understand that the problem-solving process becomes as important as the content being learned.

This approach also allows students to think creatively and become more self-directed learners. They are able to explore their own personal learning styles, and when they succeed by completing their projects it fosters a sense of self-worth, realizing they can overcome challenges that at first may have appeared insurmountable. Project-based learning requires that students solve difficult problems, which may ultimately help them become effective problem solvers and lead to a broader and more complete understanding of the subject matter.

Project Length

Educators should also think about the length of the project. If the project is too big, students might have difficulty completing it within the required time frame, or they might complete it just to get it done and miss out on valuable learning opportunities. Even at the graduate level, students often choose projects that are too complex.

It is critical to guide students through this first step in determining their project; otherwise they may get frustrated and give up right away. Markham, Larmer, and Ravitz (2003) identified a number of different types of projects—adapted for this book in table 2.2—that may be used in a variety of subject areas. There are several different types of projects identified, some of

Table 2.2. Types of Projects Adapted from the Buck Institute for Education

Written	Presentation	Technological	Media
Research report	Speech	Computer database	Audiotape
Narrative	Debate	Computer graphic	Slide show
Letter	Play	Computer program	Videotape
Poster	Song/lyric	Podcast	Drawing
Brief	Musical piece	Website	Painting
Proposal	Oral report		Sculpture
Poem	Panel discussion		Collage
Outline	Reenactment		Map
Brochure	Newscast		Scrapbook
Pamphlet	Discussion		Oral history
Survey	Dance		Photo album
Autobiography	Proposal		
Essay	Data display (e.g., chart)		
Book review	Exhibition of products		
Report			
Editorial			
Movie script			

which are more specific to particular disciplines, such as construction products for industrial technology courses, and others that are more general, such as written products that may be used in any course.

Planning the Project

Once the project has been chosen, the next step is for students to gather information they might need to start creating their project. To gather this information, students may need to conduct interviews, use the Internet, go to the library, read articles and books, and find examples of projects similar in nature that have already been completed by others.

During this phase of the project, educators may want to have students keep learning logs, which entails writing down the steps along the way and keep a running tally of the time they spend on their projects. The educator's role during this portion of the project is to let the process unfold.

Students may come to the instructor when they have questions and need assistance, but the instructor should refrain from doing the work for them. Instead, instructors should give them the needed resources, which will allow them to discover the answers for themselves that they need in order to keep moving forward.

Having students collect and save materials such as interview notes, printed material from the Internet or library, learning logs, and other information may serve as important artifacts that educators can use when assigning a grade to the student's work (chapter 5 discusses this in detail). Students should organize their artifacts in such a way that they can be turned in to the educator when the project is completed. A learning portfolio is one option that has worked well for my students.

Educators may wish to provide students with electronic documents that allow them to chart their progress as they move toward completing the project. Too much structure may inhibit students from engaging in their own problem solving when completing a project, but younger students may need more direction with specific instructions like the forms mentioned above.

POTENTIAL PROBLEMS WITH PROJECT-BASED LEARNING

I have observed teachers claiming that they are using project-based learning in their classrooms when it was obvious that they lacked an understanding of the key principles. In one particular situation, the instructor demonstrated each step of the project process, and, as the instructor demonstrated the steps, the students replicated the process. In the end, all the projects looked the same. So what did the students learn from this process?

If educators want students to learn more than how to follow directions, they must give them freedom to experiment and make mistakes. Educators must allow students to manage their time, take responsibility for their actions, and make mistakes, which will help them learn how to solve problems. Projects are the products of the process, but the instructional delivery is equally important.

Educators have a tendency to control the learning process. Lesson plans are developed, learning objectives are identified, and methods are designed to help students learn these objectives. Educators who are accustomed to using this traditional model for much of their teaching careers have a difficult time letting go of some control in the classroom. However, relinquishing control is necessary in order for students to learn life skills.

Educators need to let students initiate the learning process by allowing them to choose projects of their own interest. Educators should not step in and rescue students the minute they get stuck. They need to let students try things and test out their ideas to see if they work. This is how students learn skills that they will use long after they leave formal education.

Time is another potential problem with project-based learning. There are numerous charter schools that use project-based learning primarily because they are free from many of the state regulations. Teachers in traditional public school settings that attempt to implement project-based learning may stop because of the pressures of standardized testing and lack of time to go in-depth with the project process.

Higher-education instructors teaching lecture classes also face time constraints. They often have more freedom to implement project-based learning but need to be creative as to how they do this. If they use class time for students to work on projects, then they may need to allow several class periods for students to complete a project. Instructors that believe in depth over breadth will find ways to incorporate it into their courses. Projects allow students to go deeper in their learning, but unfortunately large lecture classes often prevent instructors from using it.

Group projects may also present a problem when using project-based learning. Educators need to think carefully about how they will use small groups in the learning process. One philosophy is to break them into groups with a maximum of four and let them determine the tasks and decide who will do each specific task.

Another option is to identify several projects and allow the groups the freedom to choose the one they are most interested in doing. The instructor should make sure that each project consists of a series of tasks that can be divided up equally among the students. This way the educators can create a better group dynamic because all members will have approximately equal amounts of work. In some cases, educators might want the group to struggle through the process of determining tasks for each member, which typically works better with older students.

Some teacher direction may be needed with younger students, but at least they are still doing project-based learning, which is better than none at all. With a little creativity, educators at all levels and in all learning environments can implement some project-based learning. It is worth the upfront time in planning and preparing because it helps students learn important life skills.

Chapter Three

Skills That Matter

When conducting presentations and workshops, parents and educators often describe what they believe are the most important skills their children should learn during their high school or college experience. They routinely include life skills such as creativity, problem solving, communication, and self-direction.

They rarely say they want their child to learn better note-taking or test-taking skills or that they want their child to be a better memorizer. The skills that matter most to parents, and employers for that matter, are not being taught in our classrooms.

Developing life skills in order to be effective professionals has been on the education radar since the early 1990s. In 1990 the Secretary of Labor put together a task force of experts consisting of educators, employees, supervisors, and business and labor leaders from across the nation to compile a report identifying the necessary skills students need to do well in the workplace.

The original report, *What Work Requires of Schools*, was published by the Secretary's Commission on Achieving Necessary Skills (SCANS) in 1991. This report identified specific skills students need in order to succeed at the workplace and in life in general. Table 3.1 shows a list of the thinking skills and personal qualities that were identified in the original SCANS report.

These skills and qualities were identified as being vitally important to the workplace; yet they continue to be sorely overlooked in the US educational system, both at the college and high school levels. Students continue to graduate lacking these types of skills that would allow them to excel in their professions. Recently there has been a resurgence for college and high school students to learn these types of skills so that they can be better prepared for life after school.

Table 3.1.   SCANS Thinking Skills and Personal Qualities

Thinking Skills	*Personal Qualities*
Creative thinking	Responsibility
Decision making	Self-esteem
Problem solving	Sociability
Seeing things in the mind's eye	Self-management
Knowing how to learn	Integrity/honesty
Reasoning	

Wagner (2008, 14–38) emphasized the importance of developing a variety of different life skills. He interviewed a number of business owners and asked them what they believed were the most important skills that students should have acquired by the time they come to work for their organizations. Through his interviews, Wagner identified a list of what he refers to as the seven survival skills that employers believe are essential for students to have once they enter the work world: problem solving, collaboration, agility, initiative, oral and written communication, assessing information, and curiosity. Employers are interested in hiring individuals who are self-directed, have the ability to ask probing questions, can solve critical problems, can be productive team players, and are able to adapt to ever-changing work environments.

Tough (2012, 75–76) conducted an extensive analysis on character development and identified a number of characteristics that would help students to succeed. He examined a number of research studies and writes about the importance of developing noncognitive traits such as gratitude, self-control, optimism, zest, curiosity, social intelligence, motivation, and grit.

These traits can help predict essential satisfaction and academic achievement and are primarily behavioral traits. The one in particular that relates to life skills is grit. Grit is similar to perseverance, which is learned through failure. When students go through multiple trial-and-error attempts at completing a task, for example, they are learning to stick with it and persevere until they complete the task to their own satisfaction.

Trilling and Fadel (2009, 7) conducted extensive research on what they call twenty-first-century skills. The skills they identify are similar to the skills identified by Wagner and Tough. Trilling and Fadel's study was conducted through the Partnership for Twenty-First-Century Skills Conference Board of four hundred hiring executives from major corporations. The study found that "students graduating from secondary schools, technical colleges, and universities are sorely lacking in some basic skills and a large number of applied skills: oral and written communication, critical thinking and problem solving, professionalism and work ethic, teamwork and collaboration, working in diverse teams, applying technology, and leadership and project management."

The skills that these researchers identified are similar to the skills in the SCANS report, but unfortunately, not much has been implemented in high school or college for students to learn these skills since the original SCANS report was published in 1991. Employers are still faced with the same problem of hiring new employees fresh out of high school or college that lack these skills.

WHAT ARE LIFE SKILLS?

There are multiple terms such as *noncognitive skills*, *people skills*, *soft skills*, *social skills*, and *life skills* that all include similar types of skills. Scholars have begun promoting the development of noncognitive skills in schools and universities, defining them as "academically and occupationally relevant skills and traits that are not specifically intellectual or analytical in nature" (Rosen, Glennie, Dalton, Lennon, and Bozick 2010, 1). Noncognitive skills appear to be less cognitive and more behavioral in nature and include things like motivation and self-control.

Noncognitive attributes are associated more with an individual's personality as opposed to his or her intellect. The same holds true for the definitions for *soft skills*, *people skills*, and *social skills*. Kamin (2013, 12), who wrote a comprehensive book on soft skills for the corporate sector, defines them as "interpersonal skills that demonstrate a person's ability to communicate effectively and build relationships with others in one-on-one interactions as well as in groups and teams. Skills include listening and responding in a receptive way to others' points of view: cooperation and the ability to be flexible and take positive action in situations that require understanding of the circumstance, environment, and the culture of the person, organization, team, or family in which specific interactions occur." This definition of soft skills is quite similar to the definitions of people skills and social skills. Here's how people skills and social skills are defined by Dictionary.com:

People skills: the ability to deal with, influence, and communicate with other people.
Social skills: the personal skills needed for successful social communication and interaction.

These definitions are centered on behavioral traits that allow individuals to work in a team atmosphere and interact positively with their peers and colleagues. They are less cognitive and more behavioral in nature.

The term *life skills* has different meanings depending on the context. Problem solving, creativity, and time management have been identified as life skills; however, there are other skills that individuals refer to as life skills. One particular author refers to things like shaking hands correctly, introducing people correctly, maintaining eye contact, and being aware of others as life skills (Pestallozi 2013, 7).

Although important, these are rudimentary skills and are not the types of skills that will be discussed in this book. The skills identified in this book are a combination of cognitive and behavioral abilities. They are skills that require students to think, analyze, and execute. Here is a list of the skills that will be referred to as *life skills* in this book and that can be learned by students when they are in learning environments using certain teaching approaches:

- Problem solving
- Responsibility
- Work ethic
- Critical thinking
- Self-direction
- Communication
- Creativity
- Collaboration
- Perseverance
- Time management

All of these skills require that students think before they act. Problem solving and critical thinking are obviously cognitive skills, but so are the rest. For instance, creativity requires students to think about how to solve problems in new ways, and perseverance is when individuals decide to continue to solve a challenging problem requiring multiple trial-and-error attempts until they reach a solution. The same holds true for the rest of the skills; they all require cognition but when executed are sometimes viewed as more behavioral than cognitive.

Some of the skills listed are the same as those identified by Trilling and Fadel (2009), Wagner (2008), and the SCANS report (1991). They are skills that individuals need in order to solve problems not only in work environments but also when encountering day-to-day problems.

Employers look for the ten life skills listed above in their new hires but continue having a difficult time finding those that possess them. Employers want to hire individuals that are creative and able to solve challenging problems. They want employees who are self-directed and can figure things out on their own. These skills are essential in today's work world yet continue to be lacking by the workforce. Why is this?

One reason is that these skills are not being taught in most college and high school classrooms. As mentioned at the outset, today's classroom emphasizes testing, which results in the use of the lecture format followed by a learning process in which students memorize information for the tests. The education system in the United States is focused on learning content, and in traditional learning environments educators begin in the present and work backward to the past. Figure 3.1 depicts how the lecture format begins in the present but moves backward to the past. Students are expected to memorize information, facts, and theories for tests. The skill being learned in this process is memorization, which may work for getting a good grade on a test. But will the information ever be applied or retained?

With this format, students learn about other people's discoveries and experiences that took place in the past. Textbooks are filled with information that others have already discovered. The goal is to cover all the content within a structured time frame and have all students in the class memorize the same information at the same time for the same tests.

What is occurring in the heads of students asked to absorb information this way? And, most importantly, is it motivating them to learn? While memorization is important, it is not one of the skills mentioned in any of the lists compiled by the research studies mentioned earlier.

Another reason students are not being taught life skills is because life skills require a significant amount of time to teach and learn. In the current education system, students are not allowed the time or freedom to work on solving challenging problems, managing their time, or learning from their mistakes.

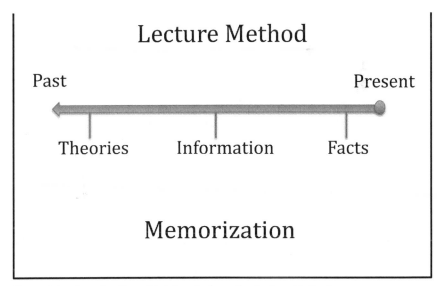

Figure 3.1. Learning Type That Results from the Lecture Method

In order to learn these skills, students must be allowed time to solve challenging problems, collaborate with peers, and follow through with their assigned tasks.

In the US education system, educators are busy trying to cover all the curriculum standards in the allotted amount of time. There is no time left for students to work on in-depth projects and explore possible solutions that would allow them to learn these skills. As one of my former graduate students said, "I agree with the philosophy of experiential learning, but as a school teacher I do not have time to implement it."

HOW DO STUDENTS LEARN LIFE SKILLS?

Students learn life skills by practicing them over and over, and in order to practice them, they must be placed in situations where they can manage their time, collaborate with peers, solve problems, and communicate their ideas with one another. They can't learn these skills by sitting in a classroom listening to a teacher talk. In-depth projects are an effective way to help students learn these skills.

While teaching at a university in Michigan, I helped facilitate a campus-wide spaghetti-bridge-building competition for undergraduate students. Among the rules for the competition: students could only use two one-pound boxes of spaghetti, ten glue sticks, and a glue gun to build their bridge. In addition, there could be a maximum of four students on each team, the bridge had to span twenty-four inches with a three-inch-wide roadbed, and the building phase had to be completed in two hours.

The objective of this project was to build the strongest bridge. A metal hook mounted to a small three-by-five-inch piece of plywood was placed in the center of the roadbed, and a plastic bucket was hung on the hook in the center of the roadbed. Once the building phase was complete, the bridges were tested for strength by adding small weights to the bucket until the bridge collapsed and the bucket fell to the floor. At the competition, the bridges were placed between two tables and the bucket hung at least a foot above the floor.

There was an initial meeting at the beginning of the spring semester in January, and the competition was held in March. This gave each team about two months to practice building bridges and to test them for strength prior to the competition. At the first year's competition, the victorious engineering team's bridge held forty-four pounds. The competition facilitators were a little nervous, as we almost ran out of weights and could not believe a bridge made from two one-pound boxes of spaghetti could hold that much weight.

During and after the competition, many of the teams were asked what they had learned from the experience, and many of the replies were similar: they had learned how to work together as a team and had figured out specific tasks for each participant so that during the competition they all knew exactly what they needed to do to maximize their efficiency.

For example, the engineering team built several jigs out of small pieces of two-by-four blocks of wood with grooves cut into them at specific lengths. This allowed team members to work on different parts of the bridge like the trusses or roadbed.

Each team member had his or her own jig and would place strands of spaghetti in the grooves of the jig and cut them into specific lengths. Some of the grooves were different widths, which held different numbers of spaghetti strands. Smaller bundles consisting of three or four strands of spaghetti were used for the trusses, whereas the thicker bundles of five or six strands were used for the roadbed. As we looked on, we could see team members performing their own specific tasks in order to work efficiently as a team.

They also learned how to manage their time. They realized they had to be fast yet precise in cutting and gluing spaghetti strands together. They learned they had to complete their tasks in a certain amount of time in order to assemble the entire bridge together.

They learned how to be responsible by showing up for each practice session prior to the competition so they could brainstorm and problem solve ways to build the strongest bridge. They learned about bridge designs and what components of certain bridges allowed them to support more weight. And they learned to be creative by building different designs and improvising to make them stronger.

One group said they learned by failing multiple times. Failing allowed the group to go back to the drawing board, come up with new ideas, create new plans, build a new bridge, and test it to see if it was stronger than the previous one they had built. This process forced them to think, reevaluate, solve new problems, be creative, become more efficient, work together, and persevere by not giving up after their first attempt.

This project was challenging, spanned a couple of months, and required multiple trial-and-error attempts before students were satisfied with their end products. Learning life skills was a by-product of the process, and they were learned during this two-month period of time.

For example, the more time students spent on the project, the more they learned how to work effectively as a team and how to solve problems they faced as they constructed their bridges. Since people need to use life skills every day as adults, why not begin teaching students these skills early on in their education?

People are constantly learning and improving their life skills. Younger people tend to have more rudimentary life skills because they have not had as many opportunities to practice them as adults have had. As individuals mature they are exposed to more complex projects and experiences.

Being a bread baker at a Panera restaurant, for example, requires skills in problem solving, communication, and responsibility. The baker will need to figure out the recipes and mix the appropriate ingredients to make good-tasting bread. The baker will need to communicate effectively when training new bread bakers or calling a supplier to order more ingredients.

Bread bakers will also need to be responsible by showing up to work on time and making sure the bread is ready when needed. The bread baker needs certain life skills to work at the restaurant. But now imagine the skills needed in order to manage this restaurant.

The manager will need a variety of life skills to manage the employees and the restaurant. Managers may need to design and create a website, convene staff trainings, hire and fire employees, resolve conflicts among employees, determine salaries, manage a budget, and design a menu. The manager must be adept at communication, responsibility, time management, problem solving, adaptability, collaboration, and perseverance. And, like bread bakers, managers will become more effective at these skills over time as they practice them.

Are students learning these skills in their classes? They will not if the education system continues to emphasize test taking. Students have a better chance at learning these skills through their jobs or by participating in extra-curricular activities.

I work for an organization called Innovative Quality Schools (IQS), which authorizes and provides oversight for charter schools. Many of these schools are implementing project-based learning, and part of the oversight process includes interviewing students about their experiences with project-based learning. Students who have been interviewed are extremely articulate and mature. Where and how do they acquire such effective public speaking and communication skills?

A couple of years ago I attended an IQS conference in Minneapolis and watched a high school student give an articulate speech and answer challenging questions afterward. After the speech, she told me how lucky she was to have attended a project-based learning school where she was continuously solving problems associated with her projects and presenting them to peers, teachers, and parents.

She also said there were multiple visitors at her school, and she would talk with them about the school and her projects. She learned to be comfortable around adults through these visits and became more effective at communicating her ideas through these experiences.

Project-based learning is an effective way for students to learn life skills. When students are engaged in project-based learning, they are immersed in projects that involve confronting numerous problems along the way. A good project includes multiple problems where students are not able to complete it in one attempt. The project must be complex enough so that students go through several trial-and-error episodes before the project is finished. This is how students learn life skills like problem solving; they must practice them over and over in order to learn them and perfect them.

Project types are endless, and the sky is the limit. High school teachers I have worked with have created a number of projects for their students. One teacher had students develop a healthy snack shop for the school. They worked as a group to figure out what types of snacks they would sell, where they would purchase the snacks, and how they would run the shop. During this process they were learning how to be responsible by completing their assigned tasks, as well as how to run a small business.

Other teachers have had students draw blueprints and construct objects from them, design community gardens, build websites, create podcasts, and design skateboard parks. Most of these projects entailed doing formal presentations in front of city councils, peers, and teachers on what they learned from these experiences. This helps students solidify their learning by expressing their ideas and explaining what they did and what they learned.

With project-based learning, students are explorers and discoverers. Students confront multiple problems as they begin to create a project. For example, the bridge building contest required multiple experiences building bridges and testing them to determine their strength.

With each experience the participating students learned something new; they built upon these experiences by trying new ideas and building new bridges. They learned not only how to build a stronger bridge but also how to think critically, how to be creative, and how to persevere. Eventually they built a bridge they were satisfied with, and the process ended.

This process of solving problems is more complex than memorizing information because it requires that students communicate by explaining why one idea would work better than another. It also requires multiple episodes of thinking and doing.

Thinking through a problem is critical, but so is the doing phase. The doing phase is often where unexpected problems crop up that require students to generate new ideas. The doing phase often takes time. For example, designing and creating a new charter school may take multiple years before it is completed.

This type of learning is powerful and has a lasting effect on students. When students do something, they tend to remember what they are learning much longer than memorizing information for tests, which is usually forgotten shortly after the test is taken.

The process is challenging and requires extra effort. The day-to-day work individuals do in their professional lives is similar in that it entails creating and completing multiple challenging projects. If this is so, then why not teach students life skills in high school and college so they are equipped with these skills, which are needed in order to be successful in their jobs?

People can gaze around their offices or homes and see all types of objects that started out as ideas and turned into projects. Tables, chairs, sofas, Blu-ray players, flat-screen TVs, iPods, computer, pictures, window blinds, windows, carpet, and more. All of these things started out as ideas and turned into projects that people continue to refine and build upon today.

For example, vinyl-insulated energy-saving windows have been created to include multiple panes filled with argon, which prevents heat from escaping and keeps the windows from fogging up, and some wooden end tables now have electrical outlets so individuals can charge their computers and other technology gadgets.

People continue to improve upon these products, making them better all the time. Products continue to evolve and improve over time, and as new products are created they are better able to meet the needs of consumers. Creativity, innovation, and problem solving are the types of skills individuals need in order to improve upon previous products.

Projects start out as ideas and turn into inventions. Individuals start with an idea and then construct it. They test it out, and if it doesn't work they refine it. Failure is part of the project process.

Washor and Mojkowski (2013, 77) say that "projects provide opportunities to pursue a single topic, issue, or challenge over time and in depth. The potential for craftsmanship is built in, as is the demand for drawing deeply on multidisciplinary competencies."

This process requires time and effort. Individuals learn how to solve problems, manage their time, take responsibility, communicate, and collaborate while engaged in in-depth projects. Even though learning takes many shapes and forms inside and outside a school, project-based learning is one of the more effective instructional strategies (Barrell 2010; Cole and Washburn-Moses 2010).

Other experiential-learning activities such as internships, apprenticeships, and community service may provide excellent learning opportunities for students. But the reason why projects are the primary focus of this book is because many times out-of-school experiences evolve into some sort of project, the by-product of this process being the acquisition of life skills.

CONNECTING LIFE SKILLS TO PROJECT-BASED LEARNING

Several years ago, I interviewed seven middle school teachers who were implementing project-based learning in their classrooms. During these interviews, the teachers' descriptions of these projects came to life. One teacher discussed how her students had created Roman coliseums and other Roman architecture using food such as cake and gelatin molds. The pictures she shared depicted the time and effort students put into their projects.

Another teacher had students create personal collages that displayed the student's interests and hobbies, which were then presented to the class as a way for students to get to know one another. In a communications class, students videotaped and presented their own puppet shows.

Other projects included building small wooden bridges to see how much weight they could hold, making small boats powered by rubber bands to see how far they could move across a small pond, creating posters featuring famous scientists, and formulating computer-generated projects like CAD drawings and PowerPoint presentations.

Teachers were asked what they thought the strengths of project-based learning were:

It promotes discussion and peer teaching, enhances student ownership, increases higher-order thinking and life skills, and promotes group cohesiveness.

Students like it because it challenges them, they are excited about it and retain more, they understand and comprehend the material, the upper-end and lower-end students work together [toward] a common goal with group work, and students like to have choice and they buy into the process.

I saw a kind of unity take place with kids. They bought into it right away because any type of activity that you get them involved in they respond [to] in a positive way.

Project-based learning basically forced the students or put them in a position where they were able to work together [toward] a common goal. That is something they don't get on a day-to-day basis and something I feel they need. They were able to achieve that through a project. (Wurdinger et al. 2007, 157–58)

One of the main themes running throughout these interviews was life skills development. Teachers witnessed that students were motivated to complete their projects and through the process were learning how to solve problems and collaborate.

I teach a graduate course called Project-Based Learning where students have created such projects as a gap-year program for Taiwanese students, a curriculum that includes project-based learning for their own students, a faculty workshop on inclusivity, a charter-school proposal that would incorporate various experiential learning approaches, and a wilderness program for Native American youth.

The course includes a number of readings about project-based learning, discussions on how to develop life skills, and examples of rubrics and assessments. The course also includes having students fill out project-proposal forms, learning logs, and reflections at different times on what they are learning from doing their projects (examples of these forms are provided in chapter 5).

At the conclusion of the course, students present their projects to the class. The course spans a sixteen-week period, and all of their projects must be complex enough to solve multiple problems during the process.

Students were asked what they were learning from their projects:

> I have learned that I am a lot better at managing my time when I have a busy schedule [than] when I don't have a lot going on. I have also learned that when I am passionate about something, I can spend a lot of time learning about it and focusing on that topic. Finally, I have realized that I am persistent when I reach a problem and become determined to find a solution.

> I'm learning about my own interests and abilities. In considering the project for this class and looking ahead to a capstone project, I take stock in what I really want to do with my life. I'm thinking about starting my own "school" based on "old world" art techniques.

> Organization is so very important. With full-time teaching and working on my [master's], I have been even more organized than usual.

> I am working on making projects more individual. It's important to let kids work at their own pace and on their own ideas and passions.

> I am learning how hard it is to tackle a big idea/project and break it down to a manageable size, as well as how to set smaller, measurable goals, which help me move forward without losing sight of the bigger goal. (Wurdinger and Qureshi 2014, 5–6)

Whether middle school or graduate school, students enjoy project-based learning because it motivates them to learn, it is challenging, and it allows them to learn meaningful skills that they can use on a daily basis. It is an ongoing process of continuous learning. When individuals engage in projects and are allowed to present them in a public forum, they are practicing life skills, and with each experience they learn to improve upon them.

In-depth projects are the way that students learn these skills. Projects have to be relevant and meaningful to students so they are motivated to follow through and complete them.

Challenging projects are necessary so students learn that failure is a necessary component of the learning process. Educators at all levels should incorporate projects into their curricula so that students have the opportunity to learn skills that will allow them to become mature adults who are able to solve difficult problems, create new ideas, and become productive, effective professionals at their workplace.

Chapter Four

Using Your Place for Student Projects

Place-based learning focuses on completing projects and has evolved over the past several years. Originally, it was directly tied to environmental education and could occur anywhere within urban, suburban, and rural contexts (Sarkar and Frazier 2008). Its primary focus was to use environmental education as a way to improve the place or community in which one lived. More recently, community has become as significant as environmental education in defining place-based learning.

According to the Place-Based Education Evaluation Collaborative, "place-based learning focuses on using the local community as an integrating context for learning at all levels" (2002, 2). Smith and Sobel (2010) suggest that it includes the incorporation of a local community's history, culture, and people, and in order for students to learn about these things they must leave the classroom and develop projects in collaboration with places like schools, colleges, organizations, and businesses within their community. Place-based learning is very similar to project-based learning, except that it has a focus on creating projects that help improve the environment and community.

Turning the place where you live into a project is not difficult. Communities are filled with needs, stories, and events that can easily be turned into projects. I once asked the late Sigurd Olson, who lived in Ely, Minnesota, and was a well-known Minnesota nature writer, if he could tell the history behind Pine Island, a tiny island located on Burntside Lake near his cabin.

Paddling out to this island and walking among the enormous white pines that had never been logged was a memorable experience. He told me that the island had never been logged because it was hidden in the middle of numerous other islands on the lake.

White pines, highly coveted for their wood, grew on this island to stupefying heights and were estimated to be between 150 and 300 years old with bases spanning two to three feet in diameter. These trees were extremely valuable in the late 1800s when logging was at its peak, but luckily they were not discovered until after the logging era had ended, allowing future generations to enjoy their beauty.

Olson's story could easily be turned into a project for students. For instance, students in a biology or history course could count the number of trees on this relatively small island, take their girth measurements to estimate their age, photograph them, create a presentation on the importance of preserving these trees, and present it at a local town hall meeting. This project would allow them to learn how to conduct research on the history of this island and the logging era, learn how to age a tree, practice photography skills, learn how to develop a verbal presentation, learn to collaborate with peers, take responsibility for completing tasks, and practice communication skills.

Reaching out to individuals that live and work in your community and asking them questions about the history and current needs of their organizations and businesses provides opportunities to create meaningful projects for students. Communities are filled with projects that not only can help educate students but can also fulfill a need and educate others who live in the community.

LOCAL PROJECTS

Following are examples of projects that students completed in my courses. These projects can be easily adapted for your own classrooms. I teach courses in experiential education and educational leadership at a university in south-central Minnesota.

Many of the students in these courses work in public, charter, and outdoor education schools. Students create projects that improve their educational environments where they work. School environments are always in need of improvements and are rich with the potential for creating a variety of projects.

The community in which they live also provides opportunities for project development, and reaching out to community members allows students to discuss potential needs. Several students that reached out to local community members in my city created wonderful projects that benefited not only the organizations but also numerous individuals associated with these organizations.

The first four projects described below were created to enhance the learning of the students at local schools or colleges. The second four projects are community projects. With these projects, students reached out to community members working in different organizations and identified a need, which their projects fulfilled.

Healthy-Snack Shop

Students in my classes have completed a number of place-based projects that evolved out of their own school environments. One teacher, for example, decided to create a contest for her students to determine what they believed was a relevant problem that needed to be fixed at their school.

The students brainstormed a list of problems, and through a process of elimination they decided that the school needed more options for healthy snacks. They voted to create a healthy-snack shop because they wanted alternatives to what was currently being offered to them at their school. Her class decided that they would create and run the shop.

This place-based project created a number of challenges and problems, which students had to overcome as they worked toward the creation of this shop, requiring a fair amount of problem solving and collaboration. Students had to find out what kinds of foods were healthy and appealing to the student body, how much they should charge for these foods, where they would purchase the food they would sell, how to create a schedule for working the snack shop, and what they would do with the proceeds.

They had to test out their ideas when they began selling food to see how to run the shop and adjust their ideas as they proceeded. This project allowed students to learn skills such as problem solving, organization, and communication.

It also allowed them to learn how to run a small business and how to take on responsibilities for doing tasks and completing them. This type of learning is more rigorous and meaningful because it has a direct impact on their lives. Students take ownership of their learning because it was their idea.

This project probably impacted their lives in other ways as well. For instance, they may have learned more about health and nutrition and changed their eating behaviors or perhaps learned more about the importance of effective communication when running a small business. These are the types of skills they need to learn in order to survive in today's world.

The process of completing this particular project required that the students consider multiple topics. Students learned about nutrition, marketing, economics, communication, and business practices, which is an interdisciplinary approach to learning. In traditional classes, educators compartmentalize subject matter and tend to break down content into small bits and pieces in order to provide students with just the necessary information they need for tests.

When students take on the challenge of creating a complex project, they need to take a broader perspective and consider a wide range of topics. Each topic creates its own set of problems to solve, and solving these problems creates a rigorous learning environment for students.

Kilowatt-Hour Cost Saving

Another student decided to create a project based on electricity use at the university. Specifically, he decided to determine the approximate cost of electricity per day in the three-story building where the courses are conducted and determine ways for the university to cut down on electrical costs.

This was a difficult, time-consuming process, and the results were not completely accurate, but they at least gave the facilities director an approximation on how to cut back on costs. The student's project was based on the electricity being used by the lights only in the classrooms. He did not include the use of technological appliances such as computers and classroom projectors.

This student enjoyed math and electricity, and he truly enjoyed working on his project. He used the following formula to determine the approximate cost of electricity when classrooms were not in use:

$$\textit{wattage} \times \textit{hours used} \div 1000 \times \textit{price per kWh} = \textit{cost of electricity}$$

In order to determine the amount of electricity being wasted, the student first decided to walk through all three floors of the building several times each day for a month and record the number of rooms with lights on that were not in use. He was able to receive a copy of the building's schedule to determine when each room was in session with classes. When he found a room that was not in use with the lights on, he assumed the lights would be on until the next class session.

This is where his methodology produced a little inaccuracy, because someone could walk past the room and shut off the lights. Each time he would walk through the halls of the building, he would multiply the wattage of each fluorescent tube by the number of minutes or hours used when the room was empty. He then divided this number by one thousand and multiplied it by the cost of electricity.

He did this for one month and averaged the total cost for one month by nine months, during which time the fall and spring semester classes were in session. He then set up a meeting with the vice president of facilities management and discussed his findings with him.

This meeting resulted in one significant change. Although the vice president of facilities left the university not long after his meeting with this student, motion-sensor lights were installed in most of the classrooms the following fall semester. This one change may have cut down costs significantly. This project took place right in the building where this student was taking his classes. He took his immediate place and turned it into an in-depth project. What did he learn from this project? When he first started the project he thought it would be fun to use his interests in math and science to calculate energy waste in the building, but once he started the project he realized there could be very practical applications for the university.

He not only learned how to conduct some research, but he also learned how to organize his thoughts into a presentation. He was able to practice research skills, organizational skills, and communication skills. This student was fairly introverted, and so the most challenging piece of his project may have been the presentation he gave to the vice president.

Historical Crayon Rubbings

One student was a history buff and created a project based on the history of the university. He spent most of his time in the library's archives, reading information about the university and writing down major events since its inception. As a way of documenting the history for his classroom presentation, he decided to walk around the university and use crayon rubbings of monuments, cornerstones, building names, and other important historical plaques and monuments.

Crayon rubbing is a simple process but effective when bringing the history into the classroom. He would take waxed butcher paper and place the waxy side down on, for example, a cornerstone date of a building and then take a crayon lengthwise and rub it over the year, creating a rubbing of the date.

Back in the late 1960s and early 1970s, this university had a lab school that was highly innovative. As part of this student's project, he asked if the students in the class could walk over to the old lab site, which has since been transformed into a day care center, and do some crayon rubbings. He wanted students to see the community garden (definitely ahead of its time) that was located in the center of the lab school and do their own rubbings of various artifacts located in this garden.

After doing their rubbings, he asked that students share their rubbings with the rest of the class. As students shared their rubbings, this student explained the history behind each artifact. This was a unique experience for all the students and made an impression on them regarding the history of the university they were attending.

At the end of this course, students presented their projects to the class in order to practice their public speaking and communication skills. His presentation consisted of showing a variety of rubbings from all over campus and an explanation of each rubbing. He walked the rest of the class through a chronological time line of all of the major events that occurred on this campus through his rubbings.

He had rubbings of building cornerstones, monuments to the Vietnam War and other major historical events, and the names of students who had tragically died in car accidents. His presentation was informative and emotional. Everyone in the class learned a great deal about this university.

The students in our program come from all across the country, but this student happened to be fairly local, coming from a town thirty miles away, so he may have been more interested in the university's history than others in the class. However, by the end of his presentation, everyone was interested in the history.

His presentation was highly creative and well thought out. This student enhanced his creative thinking skills as well as his organization and communication skills. History often gets a bad rap and is accused of being boring, but this student brought the people and places on this campus alive and captured everyone's attention in the class.

Mini Ecosystem

One of the students created a guidebook that identified all the vegetation for a small piece of property that was on the edge of the university boundary. The property was approximately seventy-five feet by seventy-five feet in size, so it was fairly small. He surveyed all the plants, bushes, and trees and created a map and a key that identified all the vegetation.

The beginning pages of the guidebook consisted of a step-by-step process that allowed individuals to identify plants, bushes, and trees on their own. The guidebook was simple to use and consisted of a process of elimination, such that if a tree did not have certain characteristics associated with its leaves or bark then the guide would direct you to another page.

The guidebook also included a key to identify animal tracks. During the time he spent on this property, he discovered that mice, squirrels, wild turkey, and whitetail deer frequently walked through this area. This student was an excellent artist, and so he drew pictures of these animals with their associated track prints next to them in the book.

The guidebook also included a section that explained the history and evolution of plant growth in immature and mature forests. Interestingly, this piece of property was a fairly mature forest because it consisted of older trees with large canopies that shaded the understory, therefore not allowing smaller plant growth to occur. The student also explained the importance of maintaining a healthy ecosystem and how interconnected and important plant and animal species are to one another.

He piloted the guidebook during his class presentation by placing each student next to a plant, bush, or tree and asked everyone to go through the process of identifying his or her vegetation using the guidebook. He asked his peers to use the guidebook with a critical eye by writing down suggestions on how to make the book easier to use.

He was pleasantly surprised to learn that his guide was fairly easy to use and that most of the students were able to identify the vegetation. The primary purpose behind his project was to teach people about the interconnectedness of the ecosystem and to engage students in discussions about how ecosystems are being threatened today by human progress.

This project was very enjoyable for this student, partially due to the fact that he had a science background. Since he was not from Minnesota, he learned about the local vegetation and wildlife. He also learned how to write a guidebook that was user-friendly for students. He practiced and honed his writing and communication skills, and he contacted publishers to learn how he might publish his book.

Dakota Uprising

For the most part, Mankato, Minnesota, has a wonderful history, excepting a particularly horrific event. Mankato was the site of the largest mass hanging of Native Americans in the United States, which occurred in December of 1862 when thirty-eight men were hung simultaneously (Lawrence 2005).

There was a large Native American population in this area back in the 1800s that the federal and state governments slowly cheated out of their land. Treaties were signed but not honored, and money was promised but never paid.

By the mid-1850s, the Native Americans could no longer maintain their way of life because they had been forced onto smaller pieces of ground with limited wildlife to hunt and were not given the money they had been promised in order to feed their families. The multiple years of false promises reached a boiling point in 1862 when four Native Americans shot and killed five settlers. This episode was the beginning of a series of killings and battles in the Minnesota River Valley where many Native Americans and white settlers lost their lives.

Several faculty members at this university have written books on this event, so one of the students read all the books, talked to one of the authors, and decided to create an interactive children's book for upper elementary students. She detailed some of the major events of the Dakota Uprising in her book in order to give students an understanding of some of the history of their own city.

My student was an exceptional artist and drew pictures of some of the key people, including Little Crow, the chief who had attempted to prevent the uprising; Henry Sibley, who was governor of the state at the time; and several others. She also drew pictures of buffalo and other wildlife to show students the connection between animals and spirituality for Native Americans, as well as what they hunted to provide food for their tribes. She left open spaces in her book for students to draw their own pictures of settlers, Native Americans, and wildlife.

She showed her book to several local elementary school teachers who asked her if she could photocopy her book so that they could use it in their classrooms. During her meetings with the schoolteachers, she felt as if she educated them on specific details of the Dakota Uprising.

Food Bank Awareness

One student, who was volunteering at a local food bank, wanted to conduct a public-awareness campaign for her project, so she spoke to the director of this organization and asked if this would be beneficial for the organization. Since the food bank—Echo Food Shelf—was not well known in the community, they decided that the campaign was a great idea and would potentially increase the amount of food donated to the organization.

And so the student created a brochure that explained the mission of the organization, as well as the specific rules that are enforced when giving away food to individuals in need. The brochure also explained how much food they give away each year and future goals for donations.

When the brochure was finished, she did a media blitz to get the word out to community organizations. She started with businesses that she thought might want to donate food, such as grocery stores, large restaurants, and bakeries. She also publicized the food bank on the local TV station and asked that businesses consider giving people discounts if they brought in a certain number of nonperishable items.

Her project was a huge success! The donations poured into the food bank. There were multiple businesses that gave discounts to those that brought in food items. To this day there are still many businesses that on certain days or during special events offer discounts if you bring food in to them.

For example, every winter the downhill ski area identifies at least one night during the winter where you receive a lift ticket discount if you bring in a certain number of food items. Since conducting that campaign, Echo Food Shelf has outgrown its building and is now located in a much larger space.

This student learned that a small brochure, along with a tremendous amount of legwork, could have an enormous impact on her community and that a significant impact could occur over a relatively short period of time. She was in our program for three years and became a familiar face in the community, meeting numerous business owners and appearing on local TV several times promoting the food bank.

Nature Center Curriculum

One graduate student identified a need in the community for the renovation and creation of new curriculum stations at a local nature center. He contacted the nature center's director and set up a meeting. The center had been in disrepair for a few years after the local school district had decided to discontinue its funding for educational programming.

The student visited the nature center, had conversations with the director, and identified a list of ideas that could result in new learning stations at the center. This student was an artist and painted beautiful wall murals with plant and animal identification activities. His enthusiasm caught on in class, and soon he had several other students helping him with this project.

During one class session, students broke into small groups and began brainstorming ideas and creating plans for different stations and began to identify specific tasks that each group would work on before the next class. The result of this brainstorming session was to create a squirrel obstacle course and create video and audio activities about birds and insects.

During the rest of the semester, they worked on these projects and slowly completed them. Through the process they learned better communication skills, how to work in teams, how to be responsible for doing their individual tasks, and how to manage their time to complete the tasks.

They also learned that it felt good to help their community provide a service that would educate young children about their natural environment. The project was such a success that some students continued to work for the nature center after the semester course had ended.

Science Museum

Mankato has a children's science museum, which continues to expand and grow in popularity. The museum moved into a bigger building, and the staff were looking for more curriculum ideas, so one student met with the museum director and asked if she was interested in having him create three indoor agricultural systems: an aquaponics system, a vermicomposting system, and a grow shelves system. She agreed, and he was off and running. He was tasked with building these systems within a given space in the museum and with a somewhat limited budget for the materials.

The aquaponics system was built with a large aquarium and grow shelves. The system works as follows: the fish produce waste, which the worms and microbes turn into fertilizer. The fertilizer is used to grow plants that are directly above the aquarium in growing shelves. The plants are typically leafy vegetables, like lettuce and kale. The plants then filter the water, which returns to the aquarium.

He built the vermicomposting system out of wood and screen material. The container has wooden slats separated by space so that air can flow into the compost material to help break down food waste. The container is filled with composting dirt, fungi, and worms.

Food waste from vegetables and fruits is placed in the container, and the worms, bacteria, and fungi break down the food waste into composting dirt. The dirt is then used in the grow shelves to grow more vegetables and fruits. The grow shelves for the vegetables and fruits are located in a different part of the museum where they are exposed to a lighting system.

After he finished constructing the three agricultural systems, he created four lesson plans to go with them. His lessons were all hands-on and included seed identification and planting seeds in small containers, worm composting using magnifying glasses to view the decomposing process, examining the differences between traditional and aquaponic growing systems, and aquaponics water testing. His lesson plans were formatted using the following headings:

Leading Question
Subject Area/General Topic
Grade Level
Learning Objective
Engage
Explore
Explain
Elaborate
Evaluate
Evoke Emotion
Materials Needed
Background Information

Most of the lesson plan headings are self-explanatory, but this student really wanted to make this a hands-on lesson, so he engaged students in his lesson plans by having them plant seeds in their own cups. In small groups, they discuss different questions and explain how they believe a seed grows.

Students also discuss questions about people without enough food to eat. His lessons are all hands-on, and his questions allow students to discuss ideas behind these three different systems.

He sent me an email about what he believed were the most important learnings from his experience working with the children's museum:

> I honed my communication skills, communicating on a very regular basis by email, phone, and in person with a program team that wanted and needed immediate response to make decisions. I learned to manage my time effectively to be available when needed for logistical support and troubleshooting. Further, I learned to create program budgets and to manage funds appropriately to maximize effectiveness of limited funds.
>
> I also gained a great deal of knowledge on aquaponics, meeting with local experts and researching [hundreds] of aquaponics designs. I learned to consider not only the most efficient aquaponics designs but also what design would work best in a museum setting.
>
> I also worked on my problem-solving skills, trying to develop a physical space and programming with limited funding and a constantly changing vision of the AgLab site by the leadership team.
>
> I developed a great deal of life skills through the implementation of this project as well as experience creating programing and specific skills on aquaponics systems. This is just a short list of what I learned. (K. Damon, personal communication, April 13, 2015)

PROJECTS OUTSIDE THE LOCAL COMMUNITY

The students in this program are mostly from out of state and are transient, in that they are usually at this university for two or three years before moving on. In one course, Experiential Learning and Education Reform, my students are encouraged to think of a place—meaning a geographic location—and organization where they might see themselves working in the future. Then they communicate with members of this organization to inquire about potential projects that the students could develop for them. Ultimately, they use these place-based projects as a vehicle to exploring potential job opportunities.

Students in this course have reached out far and wide in an attempt to help organizations with projects and to explore the possibility of employment. Since most of the students are educators, they often create curricula for these organizations.

Outdoor Education School

One student created an outdoor education curriculum that included rock climbing, canoeing, and backpacking. She researched schools in Minnesota that might be interested in integrating outdoor education into their curricula. She found a charter school called Northwest Passages in Minneapolis, drove up to the school, and proposed her curriculum to the school's director.

The timing was perfect, and the director had a background in outdoor education, so he was familiar with the content of her proposal. She was hired there directly after she graduated from our program and worked there for several years leading outdoor education trips. She left this job for another similar position located further north in Minnesota.

Science School

Another student was very excited about moving out West to live in the mountains of Wyoming. He had an undergraduate degree in biology and found a school outside of Jackson Hole called the Teton Science School, where he was interested in working. He proposed some science curriculum ideas that included hiking into the backcountry to study plants, animals, and mountain ecosystems. He too was hired directly after graduating, as an instructor for this school.

Montessori School

One student was on a mission to become a teacher at a Montessori school, so she focused all of her energy while in Mankato on researching these schools and learning about their teaching certificate program. Maria Montessori, the program's founder, believed strongly in using an active approach in the classroom, which is aligned with the philosophy of experiential learning and is the reason why this student was so attracted to these schools.

In describing Maria Montessori's philosophy, Reed (2008, 4) says she created "an atmosphere for her students in which they were free to explore and discover for themselves." My student wanted to teach elementary-age students in an environment where they were free to discover and explore on their own.

She was from California, so while she was in the process of completing her master's degree in experiential education, she decided to use the Montessori teaching certificate as her final project for our master's program. While finishing her project, she was in communication with a Montessori school in California and explained that her final project for our master's degree was the

Montessori teaching certificate. The school was very excited and hired her directly after she finished our program.

Charter School

Expeditionary Learning schools are mostly charter schools that have a learning philosophy based on using expeditions as metaphors for learning. Expeditions are typically in-depth teacher-directed projects that students complete. According to ELEducation.org, as of 2014, there were 165 schools in thirty-three states educating over 53,000 students. One student researched these schools and created a project for the class that focused on learning as much as she could about these schools and putting this information into a PowerPoint presentation that EL schools could possibly use for marketing purposes.

She contacted an EL school in Denver and interviewed the director and several staff members from this school. She also attended a conference where the executive director of Expeditionary Learning gave a keynote speech and talked with several staff members to gather more information.

During these interviews and conversations, the student began developing a relationship with several staff members from different schools and asked questions about what they looked for in people when interviewing new hires for teaching positions. When presenting this project to the class, she not only discussed the school's philosophy and practices but also talked about their hiring practices and what the school looked for in their new hires. She now works for an Expeditionary Learning school in Arizona.

STUDENT BENEFITS

Projects that are centered on a place or organization and are of interest to students have the potential to transform their lives and lead to other learning experiences. They can be implemented at both the college and high school levels but require planning on the part of the educators.

Experiences like these can change lives when they lead out into the future and inspire students to learn new things and discover new knowledge. Rigor requires that students do something with information—not just memorize it. Students need to apply information by demonstrating what they know or telling others what they know. Rigor requires students to show or tell others what they know and explain the details of a project.

Rigor should result in invigoration, where students are excited about learning and are motivated to do work on their own. Students should not need external motivation, such as a multiple-choice test, to do their homework.

They will be more excited about finding answers and solutions to problems when the learning has direct relevancy to their lives.

These projects were challenging to implement because they require students to spend time outside the classroom. However, much of the work can be completed in classroom settings, but implementing the project will eventually require them to leave school and be at the place where the project will occur. It also requires some upfront time on the educator's part. In many cases, educators will need to contact community organizations and make arrangements for the project to occur.

This approach has tremendous potential for students to learn life skills. Doing projects allows them to collaborate with peers, take responsibility, communicate with peers and community members, solve problems, and ultimately learn how to learn. If educators want students to learn important skills that they can carry with them after they graduate, then they must tap into students' interests and allow them the freedom to pursue projects that are relevant and meaningful to them.

Chapter Five

Tracking and Assessing the Project Process

Tracking and assessing student progress is important not only for instructors to evaluate projects and student performance but also to help students continue moving forward in the project process. This chapter provides a sequence that includes the use of several forms that help students stay on track and allow the instructor to evaluate the project process.

At the outset of the process, students should be provided time to brainstorm ideas with their peers as to what they want to do for a project and then identify resources they will need in order to complete the project. Tools for tracking progress might include project proposal forms, project progress forms, project completion forms, reflection forms, and self-assessments.

TRACKING THE PROJECT PROCESS

Many project based schools and programs use a variety of components to assess the project process, such as proposals, learning artifacts, and presentations. To help students organize themselves, educators should provide them with a structure that will keep them moving forward in the project process.

A project proposal form, for example, should include information such as the title of the project, the resources needed, a written plan to complete the project, a description of how the project may be applied to real-life settings, and a discussion of potential learning outcomes. Educators will need to guide students through this phase so that students identify a project that they can complete within the determined time frame.

Educators may also provide students with an artifact form that allows them to keep track of references and resources they use while working on their projects. Artifacts might include learning logs, library references, websites, list of materials needed to build the project, and drawings of the project. A form could be designed for each artifact, or a form could include all artifacts.

A third component used for assessment could be a presentation. Two individual rubrics, one for the project and the other for the presentation, could be handed out so that students know ahead of time how they will be evaluated. To help students do well, the evaluation items on the rubrics should be clearly spelled out. For instance, if the project entails building something, then a project rubric might include items such as design, length, weight, and function.

A second rubric could be fashioned around a demonstration of the project via an oral presentation and include items such as explanation of materials and design, clarity and flow of speech, and length of presentation. In addition, a reflection form could be used that includes questions about the learning process, such as: What problems did you confront while making your project? or What were your significant learnings while making the project?

In all of my courses, students complete at least one project. Depending on the course, some projects are smaller, whereas others are quite in-depth. Typically, during the first class students break into small groups and brainstorm what they might want to do for their projects. Questions from the project-proposal form below are used to help prompt their thinking and include the following: What are you most passionate about? What three questions would you like to answer while completing your project? What makes your project important to the community or world? What help might you need from experts and consultants? What resources might you need in order to complete the project? What organizations might you need to contact? What people might you need to interview?

My classes meet for three hours, so most of the first class is spent in small groups discussing these questions. However, roughly twenty minutes are used at the end to have each student present his or her potential project idea to the large group. Students are encouraged to ask questions of one another at the end of these presentations, which helps them refine their ideas.

There are several forms I use to track the project-based learning process. These forms are not meant to be busywork but, rather, to help students continue moving forward in completing the project by the end of the course. My courses meet once a week for sixteen weeks during a semester, and, depending on the course, there may be several class sessions or numerous class sessions set aside to discuss and work on projects.

For example, in Project-Based Learning, the course's main focus is for students to develop and complete one in-depth project, whereas in Teaching Methods in Experiential Learning, students complete a smaller project that focuses on curriculum development. For the purpose of explaining the tracking process, I will use Project-Based Learning as an example; however, a similar shortened version of this process is used in other courses as well.

After the first brainstorming session, an electronic version of the project-proposal form is sent to each student, which they are to fill out and bring to the next class. Below is an example of a proposal form that one student completed. AK's project that entailed developing an honor's mentor program will be used as an example of how to track the project process from beginning to end.

PROJECT PROPOSAL FORM

Student name: AK
Title of project: Honor's Mentor Program
Identify the general topic to be investigated: Mentor Programs
List at least three questions you would like answered concerning your project.

1. What type of funding could be made available for the program?
2. What duties would the mentors be responsible for?
3. Which faculty/staff would be involved in this model?

How does your project affect your life outside of school? What makes this project important to the community or world around you? This project is an ideal representation of my skills and abilities acquired through the educational leadership program. In combining knowledge gained from many classes and previous experience, I will be able to accurately demonstrate my leadership abilities. In creating a mentor program, I am taking the ready-to-be-molded program to the next level and bettering the Honors Program. This model could be used at any university, school, and/or youth camp.

What help will you need from experts/consultants?

- Professionals in mentoring programs: Center for Mentoring and Induction at MNSU
- Director of the Honors Program and administrative assistant concerning budgetary and monetary concerns
- MNSU Adventure Education Program in planning team-building activities using school resources
- MNSU Counseling Center: training for future mentors

List a minimum of three different resources you will use. At least one of these must be a person.

1. Mentor Program Coordinator, University of Houston, Franco Martinez
2. Cynthia Bemis Abrams, Leadership and PR Consulting, Bloomington, MN, City Council Member-at-Large
3. Wooden books: *Wooden on Leadership* (2005) and *Coach Wooden's Leadership Game Plan for Success* (2009)
4. Various honors-program mentorship-program models from upper-mid-west region
5. Mentoring books: *Entering Mentoring: A Seminar to Train a New Generation of Scientists* (2005) and *Students Helping Students: A Guide for Peer Educators on College Campuses* (2010)

Develop an outline or time line to define and organize your project. List the tasks/activities/steps needed to complete this project. (If the project is a group project, identify the activities each person is responsible for completing.)

1. Evaluation of current mentor program: the good and bad
2. A symbiotic relationship of honors and a mentor program: how each would benefit from the other
3. Taking the first steps: building a model
4. Evaluating obstacles and challenges to the model
5. Creating the final product using input from resources and reflections
6. Synthesizing information into presentation format: for class and presentation to honors faculty and staff

List at least three different types of resources that you will use for your project other than the Internet. Make sure to talk to a person as one of your resources.

1. Leadership and PR/consulting professional and city council member
2. Coaching and leadership books
3. Mentor Program models provided by upper-midwest-region universities

What will be your final product(s)? (Examples: report, poster, Power-Point presentation, model, article, etc.)

1. PowerPoint or Prezi
2. Organizational structure model

Tentative timeline:

March 1: contact primary resources, receive feedback, read book materials
March 2–28: Basic outline development
March 28: Review models of other programs
March 30: First draft of model
April 13: Draft revisions
April 20: Final draft

Proposal approval:
Instructor _____ Date _____
Student _____ Date _____

AK's project proposal form was well developed, and during a discussion with her about the project it was agreed that she would be able to complete it by the end of the semester. During this time, AK was working in the honors program as a graduate assistant at the university, so this project was not a simulated activity for her.

She actually intended to create this project for the university—or for another university if offered a job elsewhere. Interestingly, while she was working on this project she presented the concept at a conference in Iowa, and someone from the University of Iowa asked her to get in touch with him after she graduated because he was interested in hiring her to run this program.

The next step in the sequence is to talk with students about the details of their proposal forms, which is done during the second class session. Asking them questions about their ideas, resources, and time lines is extremely helpful.

It is also important to discuss the depth of the project and raise questions and concerns about whether the project is too thin or too large. If the project is too thin, we discuss how to make it more in-depth, and if it is too large, we discuss options such as doing a different project or completing as much as they can prior to the end of the semester, realizing they won't be able to complete it in its entirety.

In some cases, there are students who are passionate about doing larger projects and understand they will not be able to complete it by the end of the course. In these situations, students are allowed to turn in what they have completed by the end of the semester.

This usually creates a situation in which students are extremely interested in completing the project after the course ends because they have invested a significant amount of time in it. They are allowed to do these larger projects because having them work on something they are passionate about as opposed to doing it as an academic exercise is much more enjoyable.

After these discussions, students are off and running. One simple way to track their progress is to have students report out verbally during class sessions, focusing on what they have accomplished and what they need to do yet to complete their project. This encourages them to take responsibility for continuing to work on their projects each week and allows time for networking with other students who might have ideas on how to improve their project.

The primary purpose for having them report back throughout the semester is to provide an opportunity for them to receive feedback from one another, which they can incorporate into their projects. Students are great resources for one another and often provide feedback that helps improve each other's projects.

In larger classes they break into small groups of three or four and report out to their group for feedback. This works well in allowing them to have longer in-depth discussions with each other.

In addition to the verbal reports, students complete several project progress forms during my Project-Based Learning course. Much like the verbal report in class, these forms allow students to keep track of what they have done and what they still need to do to complete their project.

It helps keep them on track to finish the project by the end of the semester and allows instructors to track progress each week to determine whether students are progressing toward completion. Below is an example of one of AK's project progress forms completed toward the end of the semester.

PROJECT PROGRESS FORM

Artifacts:
Number of minutes/hours you worked on the project outside of class: 3 hours
List articles, book titles, and authors used.
Komives, S. R., Dugan, J. P., Owen, J. E., Slack, C., Wagner, W. (2001) *The handbook for student leadership development.* San Francisco, CA: Jossey-Bass.
Still reading this book. Great reference for leadership models.
Titles of videos used: N/A
Provide notes from conversations and/or interviews conducted.
HY, Honors Advising director, University of Iowa
At the Upper Midwest Regional Honors Conference, I spoke with AS, director of the honors program at the University of Iowa and vice president of the National Collegiate Honors Council, about potential jobs in honors. When I referenced a desire to develop peer mentorship in our honors program

at MNSU, he listed H—— as an information source at their university. I emailed her early Monday, March 30, asking for her advice.

Hello H,
My name is AK, and I am the graduate assistant to the honors program at Minnesota State University–Mankato. I am contacting you in reference to your Honors at Iowa peer-advising and mentorship program. I spoke to AS, and he referenced your name this past weekend at the regional honors conference in relation to this topic. I am currently working to develop a strategic plan to expand our peer-mentorship program at Minnesota State–Mankato for the future. I would love to correspond with you or any of the peer advisors about our developing program and hopefully receive some helpful advice! Our program is much smaller than Honors at Iowa; we have about 120 students. Currently we have eighteen mentors, and they assist and run various student activities and our fall retreat. The training for mentorship is minimal, and a student simply needs to take a one credit—[the] "Developing Your Mentor Philosophy" class. I am curious about the "basics" of your advising and mentoring program. What does the organizational structure look like, and how are these various positions filled? What type of training [do] the mentors and advisors complete? I hope we can continue this conversation, as your experience and knowledge from a successful program would help our future mentor program have a solid ground to stand on. Thank you for reviewing this email, and I look forward to your response.

Thank You,
AK
Honors Program Graduate Assistant
Minnesota State University, Mankato

EW, assistant director for First Year Program, Iowa State University
I met EW at the Upper Midwest Regional Honors Conference, and we spoke mostly about first-year-student retreats and the benefits to these types of events. I was meant to share presentation time and serve as a panel on first-year-student retreats, but there were some technical difficulties early in the morning, so I offered my presentation time to that student from another university. I was still able to make a connection with Emily, and she shared with me job descriptions associated with the mentor and advising programs at Iowa State University. Those documents will be used as reference in this planning and are attached at the end of this work phase form.

Websites used:

http://nchchonors.org/jobs/
http://honors.uiowa.edu/academics/honors-advising
http://www.honors.iastate.edu/uhp/leadership.php

List materials needed to build the project.

1. Computer with word-processing, Internet, and email capability
2. Access to documents from various honors programs
3. Information and resources about organizational models

Drawings, plans, blueprints, descriptions, and other resources used for your project.

*   FHP leader job description, University Honors Program (Iowa State University)
*   Overview
*   Leaders for the first-year honors program work in coleader teams to facilitate a HON 121 seminar section. With the supervision and support of the undergraduate assistants and the university honors office staff, leaders plan their section's syllabus and activities related to their section. Together with their coleader, they lead discussions, plan events, attend lectures, and facilitate group activities for their section. Leaders also attend the FHP retreat and assist with various retreat events. All leaders attend training sessions in the spring semester and also enroll in HON 302 in the fall semester to provide ongoing development, training, and support from the UAs and honors staff.

Supervision

*   FHP leaders are supervised by the undergraduate assistants and are responsible to the assistant.
*   Director of the university honors program, who reports to the administrative director of the university honors program. FHP leaders are representatives of the university honors program.

Responsibilities

*   FHP leaders hold many responsibilities, including the following:
    *   Attend all leader training sessions, including the mini-retreat
        *   Mini-retreat: Friday, February 20, 2015, 5:00 p.m.–11:00 p.m.
        *   I: Saturday, February 21, 2015, 9:00 a.m.–12:00 p.m.
        *   II: Saturday, February 28, 2015, 9:00 a.m.–12:00 p.m.
        *   III: Saturday, April 11, 2015, 9:00 a.m.–12:00 p.m.
    *   Attend HON 302 in fall semester, including one training session the Sunday before classes begin and one later in the semester

- Presemester training and kickoff: Sunday, August 23, 2015, 1:00–7:00 p.m.
- Mid-semester training: Sunday, September 20, 2015, 2:00–4:00 p.m.
○ Work alongside coleader to lead HON 121 section for two hours per week throughout fall semester
○ Meet with coleader at least one hour per week to plan section activities
○ Work with coleader to create a syllabus of semester's activities and plans
○ Assist FHP members with program components such as the degree-program assignment
○ Attend the first-year honors retreat and assist with retreat activities
  - Friday–Saturday, October 9, 2015, 2:00 p.m. on Friday to 4:00 a.m. on Saturday
○ Attend the first-year honors showcase event
○ Act as a liaison between FHP members and the honors staff as needed
○ Other duties as assigned

Skills/Abilities
A strong candidate for the leader position should possess a variety of skills, including:

- Strong work ethic
- Good time management skills
- Positive attitude
- Strong communication skills
- Ability to think creatively
- Flexibility

Length of Appointment

- Leaders will participate in leader training during the spring 2015 semester and then lead an HON 121 section in the fall of 2015.

Compensation

- Leaders receive two hours of academic credit for HON 302. Credit is applied during fall semester at the completion of the leader position.

For questions regarding the position, please contact _____.

Undergraduate Assistant Job Description (Iowa State University)
University Honors Program
January 2015 to December 2015

Overview
Undergraduate assistants (UAs) within the University Honors Program work
together along with the honors staff to provide guidance, support, and coordination for the first-year honors program. Under the guidance and supervision
of the assistant director for the first-year honors program, the undergraduate
assistants help to hire, train, and supervise the FHP leaders as well as assist
with the overall coordination of the first-year honors program, including the
honors retreat.

Supervision
Undergraduate assistants are directly responsible to the assistant director of
the university honors program, who reports to the administrative director of
the university honors program. UAs also assist the office coordinator and
department secretary as needed with duties specific to the first-year honors
program. Undergraduate assistants are representatives of the university honors program.

Responsibilities
Undergraduate assistants assist with the overall coordination of the first-year
honors program, including specific duties such as:

- Assisting with interviewing and hiring seventy-two FHP leaders
- Assisting with planning and executing spring training sessions (including
  the mini-retreat and Training I, II, and III) and fall training sessions (in-
  cluding the August and September trainings)
- Attending weekly FHP planning meetings with other staff members
- Staffing an average of ten hours per week
- Planning and coordinating the honors retreat, including chairing a retreat
  committee
- Coleading weekly Honors 302 class periods alongside other staff members
  to provide ongoing support and training for the FHP leaders
- Providing administrative support for a variety of FHP required documents,
  including FHP assignments and leaders' syllibi
- Acting as a liaison between FHP leaders and the honors staff as needed
- Other duties as assigned

Skills/Abilities

A strong candidate for the undergraduate assistant position should possess a variety of skills, including:

- Strong work ethic
- Good time management skills
- Positive attitude
- Strong communication skills
- Strong interpersonal and facilitation skills
- Ability to think creatively
- Ability to be flexible

Length of Appointment

Appointments for the undergraduate assistant position are from January to December.

Compensation

Undergraduate assistants receive payment for their position on a biweekly basis. Undergraduate assistants are paid $7.25/hour, which roughly translates to $2500 for the calendar year.

For questions regarding the position, please contact EW at _____.

With this example, AK listed a variety of artifacts including books, websites, letters, and job descriptions that she used in the process of completing her project. The project progress form is basically a list of different artifacts that students identify and document as they go through the project process.

Students fill out a new form each week during the second half of the semester, but another option is to have students continue to add new artifacts each week to their form. A different colored font could be used each week to show what new artifacts have been added from the prior week.

These forms are especially useful for students in our master's program because a portfolio is required of them at the end, and they include many of these artifacts in their portfolios. During the first half of the semester, students report out verbally on their projects, and during the latter half students submit these forms each week, which helps them document and keep track of their learning for later use when they begin to create and build their portfolios.

During the first half of the semester, students discuss their project topics and progress in small groups and report out verbally because it is not unusual for them to alter the focus of their project or change them altogether. It is important to have them break into small groups and discuss their projects with each other and then report out because it helps them refine their ideas. Filling out project progress forms without definitely knowing what they are doing for their project is a waste of time.

After solidifying their project ideas, students move forward in the process and work toward completing them by the end of the semester. At the end of the project, students fill out a project completion form. This form is given to students at the end of the process and asks them to check all artifacts that apply and allows them to pick the artifacts they feel are important to be attached to the form. In the example that follows, AK chose to include her time log, outline of the project, final product, which was a Prezi presentation, and bibliography.

PROJECT COMPLETION FORM

Final project checklist (Check all that apply, and place them at the bottom of this form):

  X   1. Time log

  X   2. Documentation of Learning

  X   3. Web/Outline

_____ 4. Report/Writing Piece

  X   5. Final Product/Visual (Poster, PowerPoint, Prezi, other)

_____ 6. Student Assessment

_____ 7. Teacher Assessment

_____ 8. Project Rubric

_____ 9. Budget

  X   10. Bibliography

Final project approval:

Student Signature AK   Date 4/27/15

Instructor Scott Wurdinger   Date 4/29/15

Project Team (if applicable)

_____   Date

_____   Date

_____   Date

Number of Documented Hours 34   Letter Grade Earned _____

Project Rubric _____   Assessment Score _____

Time log:

Project Time Log

Week	What	Hours
1	Proposal form	1
2	Work phase	4
3	Work phase	5
4	Work phase	4
5	Work phase	3
6	Work phase	4
7	Work phase	3
8	Work phase	5
9	Format presentation and reflection form	5
	Total	34

Outline:

The Honors Program: What is it?

Key Terms: What terms are unique to this program?

Program Foundation: The underlying foundation; guides other aspects

1. Mission and values: University, honors, and peer-mentor program
2. Research: Benefits of peer interaction, learning community benefits, programs with curricular components successful, and reflection to make an experience valuable
3. Learning outcomes: Of mentors, mentees, and how this is assessed

Staff and Resources: People and finances needed to help sustain the program

1. Organizational structure
2. Professionals, students, additional stakeholders
3. Financial: No additional funding at this time

Program Components: The core makeup of the training program

1. Commitment: Mentor time dedication
2. Requirements: Training, education, and development
   a. Training: Skill-enhancing activities
   b. Education: Classes
   c. Development: Activity experiences
3. Phases: Fall and spring
4. Credentials: Mentor recognition

A look to the future: After year one and the first group of mentors has been trained

1. Organizational structure
2. Job duties: Of mentors
3. Additional ideas: To add as components to program

Final Product: Prezi. https://prezi.com/pn4tqh8cwgp2/honors-peer-mentor-program/

Bibliography:
1. Kolb, D. A. (1984). *Experiential learning.* Englewood Cliffs, NJ: Prentice-Hall.
2. Komives, S. R., Dugan, J. P., Owen, J. E., Slack, C., Wagner, W. (2001). *The handbook for student leadership development.* San Francisco, CA: Jossey-Bass. Simpson, S., and Hsieh H. (2003). *The leader who is hardly known: Self-less teaching from the Chinese tradition.* Oklahoma City: Wood 'N' Barnes Pub.
3. Komives, S. R., Longerbeam, S. D., Owen, J. E., Mainella, F., and Osteen, L. (2006). A leadership identity development model: Applications from a grounded theory. *Journal of College Student Development,* 47, 401–18.
4. Lenning, O. T., and Ebbers, L. H. (1999). The powerful potential of learning communities: Improving education for the future. *ASHE-ERIC Higher Education Report,* vol. 26, no. 6. Washington, DC: George Washington University Graduate School of Education and Human Development.
5. Pascarella, E. T., and Terenzini, P. T. (2005) *How college affects students: A third decade of research.* San Francisco: Jossey-Bass.
6. Roberts, D. C., and Ullom, C. (1990). *Student leadership program model.* College Park, MD: National Clearinghouse for Leadership Programs.
7. Zimmerman-Oster, K., and Burkhardt, J. C. (1999). *Leadership in the Making: Impact and insights from leadership development programs in U.S. colleges and universities.* Battle Creek, MI: W. K. Kellogg Foundation.

STUDENT ASSESSMENTS

Although the two forms mentioned above are used for assessment purposes, there are two other forms used for self-assessments: the personal reflection form and the student assessment questionnaire. The personal reflection form consists of five questions that students address.

They address the content and skills that they learned, how the project affected them on a personal level, and the benefits and problems they encountered. The second question is of particular interest to this book because students address the skills they learned, which typically center on the eight life skills I mentioned in chapter 2.

AK's response to the second question is common of many students. She listed communication, creativity, flexibility, and work ethic as the skills she practiced and learned during the process. Other students identify problem solving, critical thinking, responsibility, time management, collaboration, and self-direction as practiced and learned during the process.

Life skills tend to be listed frequently under this question because students must interact with a number of professionals to gain knowledge and become creative problem solvers as they go through numerous trial-and-error attempts while completing their project.

Life skills development permeates this class and is often mentioned on the forms, in the assessments, and in class discussions. It is obvious that these skills are being practiced in this course because of how frequently they come up during discussions.

Reflecting on these questions and writing down their responses helps students solidify their learning. AK's personal reflection form for her honors peer-mentoring project can be found below.

PERSONAL REFLECTION FORM

Name: AK
Date: 4/27/15
Title of the Project: Honors Peer Mentor Program
What were some of the most interesting and important facts you learned about your topic?

- The people I reached out to for assistance were all very willing. They responded quickly, happy to help, and would like to know the final product. Never be afraid to reach out and network.
- Peer mentor programs exist in many forms and are unique to each location. Although they are different everywhere, the programs that encourage peer mentorship agree that they are beneficial and useful (universities, honors programs, and youth camps).
- It is hard to narrow down what ideas, activities, and training will be included. Opening up to the idea that implementation will take more than a year, the "must-haves" to the first step became clearer.
- Funding for new positions and programs is an extensive process and makes the program harder to support. Starting out using resources already available shows flexibility and makes the program more feasible in the near future.
- Peer-mentor skill development is more effective if learned and practiced. The T.E.D. acronym—Training (skill enhancing and knowledge transfer),

Education (academic courses taken), and Development (immersive experiences).
- Although leaders can exist without a formal title, naming positions and phases in training increased student interest.

What specific skills did you learn, practice, or master while working on your project?

- Communication: Engaging with experts and those who had knowledge that I did not helped to form a solid foundation for this program.
- Creativity: Besides the presentation itself, creating a program that used resources already available while still making something new was a challenge.
- Flexibility: Setting up meeting and presentation times with experts or those who would be invested in this project was difficult. I also received feedback about ideas and had to incorporate those changes with my idea of a successful program.
- Work ethic: Some weeks had fewer meetings with experts, so new information had to come from readings. It was easy to make progress after a discussion with an expert. Motivation to read and sift through material that would be valuable was low, but once the framework was established my passion for this project soared.

How has working on this topic affected you as a student, citizen, and/or member of your family?

- As a student it has allowed me to take pride in completed work because I feel this project is successful. It made me more confident in reaching out to resources that have knowledge that I do not possess.
- As part of an organization, it has increased my work satisfaction. I have been asked to extend my studies at MNSU in order to implement this program and see it through the first year. Acknowledgment of a successful and beneficial project is rewarding especially when I have been encouraged to write about the program development and submit to a journal.

What went well during your project? Explain why it went well.

- The people I contacted for resources were extremely helpful and encouraging. I gained a lot of new information about a topic in which I was previously a novice. I believe that networking and asking for help can be hard, but people that work with peer mentor programs are very willing to give advice and help those who ask for assistance.

- The organization was welcoming to the idea and provided me with access to resources and documents. I believe I expressed the need to develop a mentor program in a professional manner and explained that I would only use what resources are available now, which made it easier to support.
- Synthesizing the information into a presentation format to produce an understandable outline of the program's foundation was successful. Creating a presentation helped me to organize my thoughts and write down what aspects are the most important.

What did not go well during the completion of your project? Explain your answer.

- I believe an area that I could have improved upon was outlining the steps for the second year more clearly. Once I had narrowed down what will happen in the first year, the second year took a backburner to presentation format. I wanted to make sure that the first year was solidified and understandable to those I present this to. In doing so, time slipped by fast. Although it is unfortunate that a clear picture of the future is not in this project, it leaves room for flexibility. The mentors and mentees have the ability to shape the future of the program as they see fit.
- I wish that I would have connected with more students, faculty, and staff during the Upper Midwest Regional Honors Conference to discuss their peer mentor and advising programs. I did not foresee that I would be busy with hosting duties, so the opportunities for interaction diminished.

The other tool used to assess student learning is the student assessment questionnaire. This tool is a thirty-five question self-assessment, and each question is associated with one of eight life skills: problem solving, self-direction, creativity, work ethic, collaboration, communication, responsibility, and time management.

The tool is used as a formative assessment because students take it before the course begins and then again on the last day of class. The first questionnaire is used to identify a baseline of these skills prior to taking the Project-Based Learning course. The questionnaire uses a Likert scale in which students rank themselves:

1 = Poor
2 = Fair
3 = Satisfactory
4 = Good
5 = Excellent

Here is a sample of five questions:

1. How do you rank yourself at completing projects on time?

   1   2   3   4   5

2. How do you rank yourself as a problem solver?

   1   2   3   4   5

3. How do you rank yourself at setting goals?

   1   2   3   4   5

4. How do you rank yourself at finding new solutions to problems?

   1   2   3   4   5

5. How well do you share your ideas with others?

   1   2   3   4   5

Question one is associated with time management, questions two and four are associated with problem solving, question three with self-direction, and five with collaboration. After completing the second questionnaire, students can compare the two and determine if there were areas of growth in any of the life skills over the sixteen-week semester.

The total scores for both questionnaires are tallied to determine overall growth. Here is an example of AK's overall growth from the beginning to the end of the course.

Name	Prequestionnaire Score	Postquestionnaire Score	Change
AK	141	160	+19

STUDENT PRESENTATIONS

Presentations are extremely useful when assessing projects. I always have students present their projects to their peers at the end of the semester. College students enjoy these presentations because they are opportunities for them to teach their peers about their own personal experiences with different strategies, techniques, and applications that they have experimented with in the process of completing their projects.

According to Quay and Quaglia (2004, 5), when students do presentations it forces them to make personal connections with the material to try to understand what it means to them, which encourages them to become self-directed learners. When students do presentations, they have to figure out how to connect ideas and experiences in a sequence that makes sense to them, which helps them understand the importance of learning how to learn. Of the eight life skills discussed in this book, self-direction is arguably the most important life skill one can learn because it allows one to learn how to learn.

Other researchers also suggest that presentations help students learn a variety of life skills. For example, Thurneck (2011, 19) mentions that student presentations promote belongingness, motivation, responsibility, creativity, curiosity, and ownership of the material. Kagesten and Engelbrecht (2007, 313) conducted a qualitative study through questionnaires and interviews with students and teachers about student presentations on mathematics and found that students thought their communication skills and problem-solving ability had improved; they write, "Our study seems to indicate that this kind of teaching can create a base for active and deep learning, and it motivates students to become actively involved in the learning process."

Sander and Sanders (2005, 28) conducted an action research study with undergraduate students and found that a host of benefits arise from doing student presentations, including an increase in autonomy and independent learning, team skills, testing of knowledge, critical evaluation, and real-life application.

Girard, Pinar, and Trapp (2011, 84) surveyed 220 students that took courses in which they had to do two presentations. The students were from two universities, and the courses were in the field of business. Students were surveyed at the beginning and end of the course after all the presentations were finished. The results of these surveys indicate that presentations contributed to their learning of class materials, development of listening skills, and improved public speaking skills.

Presentations are the culminating experience of the project that allows students to practice their communication and critical thinking skills. In many programs and project-based classes, students are able to practice critical thinking skills because their peers are allowed to ask thought-provoking questions that they must answer on the spot.

Presentations not only enhance life skills development, they also provide a mechanism to assess knowledge and skills gained through the process of completing their projects. In my Project-Based Learning course, rubrics are used to assess the quality of the project as well as the quality of the presentation.

Project presentations help students organize their thoughts, express their ideas and opinions, and reflect on the important things they have learned during the process. Project presentations are different from many typical classroom presentations because students are able to speak from direct experience about the subject matter of their project.

Direct experience with the project allows them to comprehend and speak more intelligently about it because they tested their ideas in real-world settings. A project presentation helps them learn to organize their experience and put it into words that will hopefully be understood by their audience.

Certain charter schools across North America that use project-based learning rely heavily on project presentations, which they often refer to as exhibitions, to evaluate student learning. The Metropolitan Regional Technical charter school in Providence, Rhode Island, uses exhibitions as an assessment tool.

Littky and Grabelle (2004, 7), intricately involved in this school, described exhibitions as "kids getting up and talking passionately about a book they've read, a paper they've written, drawings they've made, or even what they know about auto mechanics. It is a way for students to have conversations about the things they have learned."

Other charter schools such as the ones created by EdVisions also have their students do exhibitions after completing their projects. They hold exhibitions about every six weeks where the public is invited to the school to listen to student presentations on their projects.

They also have students do a major exhibition after completing their senior projects, which usually require three hundred to four hundred hours of research. When students do exhibitions, they "take their projects more seriously, they get valuable practice speaking in public, the parents better understand the learning process, the public knows the school is serious about academics, and it builds community" (Newell 2003, 14).

Some charter schools have presentation nights once or twice a year, which allow a larger number of students to present their projects to peers, parents, and community members. These events are identified early in the school year so that students know when they will be presenting, and it allows parents and community members to place these dates on their calendars.

The time frame for presentations is important to consider, as some classroom educators may not be able to afford giving up several class periods in order for students to do presentations. But short presentations are better than none at all. Having students present their work after they complete it helps solidify their learning and provides an opportunity to practice and learn important life skills.

Providing structure to the project-based-learning process is important because it helps students understand the sequence of creating and completing
a project that has worth to them and the greater community. This sequence
requires students to report out periodically to their peers in small and large
groups, fill out different forms, do in-class presentations, and assess their own
learning. This process helps them take responsibility for their own learning
and provides multiple opportunities to learn how to communicate effectively,
be creative problem solvers, manage their time, and collaborate with peers.

Chapter Six

Schools Using Project-Based Learning

el? do?

One is more likely to find project-based learning being used as a system-wide method in high schools than in colleges. High schools, especially charter schools, tend to have a smaller number of students enrolled and are free from many state regulations, which allows them to implement innovative approaches.

Teachers in mainstream traditional schools also use project-based learning, but it is rare to find mainstream schools that use project-based learning on a system wide level. The high schools mentioned in this chapter use project-based learning as a primary teaching method throughout their entire systems. All teachers in these schools are well versed on how to implement project-based learning in their learning environments.

The use of project-based learning in colleges, on the other hand, tends to be found within certain departments or programs. Colleges and universities have numerous departments and faculty members with typically much larger student populations than charter schools.

Project-based learning tends to be found in business and engineering programs, perhaps because employees in these professions are often working on specific projects on a daily basis. The colleges and universities mentioned in this chapter were discovered by reading books on project-based learning and by doing Web searches. The departments or programs in these schools have identified project-based learning as a primary teaching approach used by their faculty.

Readers should understand that this is not an exhaustive list of colleges and schools using project-based learning. Instead, the chapter highlights a few exemplary colleges and high schools using project-based learning across the country.

COLLEGES USING PROJECT-BASED LEARNING

Westminster College

One college on the cutting edge of integrating project-based learning through-out its undergraduate and graduate programs is Westminster in Salt Lake City, Utah. This college has 161 full-time faculty members with thirty-nine undergraduate programs and thirteen graduate programs. While interview-ing President Brian Levin-Stankevich on May 23, 2013, I asked him several questions about how the college was using project-based learning.

He mentioned there are four degree programs that have changed their credit-based curriculum to a project-based one: Master's of Business Admin-istration, Bachelor of Business Administration, Master's of Strategic Com-munications, and Bachelor of Science in Nursing. Although there are only four programs that exclusively use project-based learning at Westminster, he mentioned that the college is increasing its use of project-based learning in a variety of forms across the disciplines.

Students move through these programs by completing five sequences that are roughly one semester each. Each sequence requires students to complete several projects, with the fifth sequence culminating in a capstone project that incorporates all the previous sequences.

Students work together in cohorts, but they also must work individually to complete different parts of their projects. Professors act as coaches and men-tor the students through the project process, providing them with feedback and information needed to help them continue moving forward in the process. There are typically one or two faculty assigned as coaches for each cohort.

These four programs are competency-based, and students are assessed pri-marily using rubrics that focus on life skills such as problem solving, collabo-ration, and communication, to name a few. In traditional seat-based courses that meet on a routine schedule, students are given a certain number of credits accrued toward their graduation requirements, whereas competency-based courses are designed with the goal of helping students develop employment skills.

These courses provide students with a less structured schedule, allowing them to collaborate and communicate with each other on how to complete their projects. Students work independently and together with the guidance of their professors utilizing a combination of online and face-to-face meetings.

Students must acquire certain levels of proficiency in these skills while completing a project in order to move on to the next sequence. Coaches and peers encourage each other to put forth the effort needed, which will enable the team to move forward to the next sequence phase.

The process of switching from a seat-based format to a project-based one has required a significant amount of work and has helped create a different type of culture at Westminster. Professors are no longer standing in front of the class lecturing and giving tests.

Instead they provide students with the project parameters, much like in a business setting, and then help them progress through the process of completing their projects. Students are given much more freedom and must be responsible for completing their projects.

This process promotes life skills development. Students are learning much more than content; they are learning skills like communication and problem solving, which they are assessed on during and after each sequence.

President Levin-Stankevich was extremely enthusiastic explaining the project-based learning programs and how he feels the college is moving in a unique direction focusing on student learning that is centered on learning important life skills needed for the workplace.

Olin College

Olin College, located in Needham, Massachusetts, is one of only a few colleges that use projects extensively throughout much of their curricula. The Olin website says, "Our campus culture values engagement and learning, no matter where it happens. Each semester we celebrate student work at the Olin Expo, where students share the project they are most excited about."

During my interview with Dr. Richard Miller on May 30, 2013, president of Olin College, he talked about how the college uses experiential learning, which often culminates with projects as end products. He discussed a concept called *design-based learning*, which includes a fairly lengthy process.

Students begin by identifying a group of people, usually working in a business or organization, whose lives they would like to improve at their worksite. If the individuals at the worksite agree, the students spend several days observing and questioning them on potential ideas that could help them improve their work environment. The students develop a sociological profile and then discuss this profile with the group to help identify potential projects.

This process results in the development of a meaningful project or projects that will help improve the group's work environment. Olin students become engaged in this process because they have developed working relationships with these individuals and because they realize how the project can improve the worksite.

President Miller mentioned that there are forty-two full-time faculty members working at Olin, and at least 50 percent of them are using project-based learning in their courses. Even though there are some faculty members who do not use project-based learning, they all promote experience-based learning where students are engaged in direct experiences outside the four walls of a classroom.

One of the most unique aspects of Olin's curriculum is SCOPE, which stands for Senior Capstone Project in Engineering. In the SCOPE program there are typically five to seven senior students that work in multidisciplinary teams on intensive full-year projects with partnering corporate sponsors. SCOPE is the culmination of Olin's project-based curriculum where students work closely with clients to develop projects that have value to the sponsors, who, in return, provide students with enduring educational experiences.

There are usually around thirty corporate sponsors each year that are involved in the SCOPE Program. Corporate sponsors pay the SCOPE program $50,000 to have a group of students work on these projects. Students are responsible for overseeing the budget and use this money for research and development, materials, and field trips that allow them to collect information needed to complete their projects.

President Miller was extremely excited when he was explaining Olin's curriculum and innovative approaches they are using at the college. He told me a story about a professor who teaches a history course and uses the life of Paul Revere to discuss metallurgy.

He explained that the subject becomes more interesting and real when educators attach human beings to subject areas. Students are more interested and engaged when they are learning about the trials and tribulations of other human beings as opposed to learning content that is abstract and detached from human conditions.

He is concerned about the overemphasis on passive learning and the use of lectures in higher education and stressed the importance of creativity and passion in the learning process. Developing life skills such as problem solving and innovation are at the forefront of Olin's mission, and this is evident by the number of students acquiring well-paying jobs after they graduate.

Worcester Polytechnic Institute

During my conversation on June 30, 2015, with President Laurie Leshin from Worcester Polytechnic Institute (WPI), she mentioned that students complete three significant projects during their four years of college: a humanity and arts project, an interactive qualifying project (IQP), and a major qualifying project (MQP). Typically the humanity and arts project is completed during the sophomore year, the IQP during the junior year, and the MQP during the senior year. In addition, freshman students enroll in the Great Problems Seminar where they learn about the project-based learning process and complete a project of their own.

WPI has been using project-based learning for forty years and has created over forty project centers around the world where students can engage real-world problems often identified by the project center. Typically one or two faculty will take four to six teams of four students to a project center and guide students through their project at these project centers.

President Leshin indicated that WPI changes its academic calendar during these three different projects so that students can focus their studies on one of these projects. Students take other courses during their four years of college, but certain terms, which consist of four to seven weeks, are designated for students to work on one of these three projects. Faculty that teach more traditional courses also use project-based learning in these courses so students are engaged in project-based learning throughout much of their four-year degree at WPI.

When students complete their projects, often in teams of four to six students, they present them to some of the professionals located at these project centers. For example, as WPI's website states, they might present their project to an investor on Wall Street or a computer software programmer in Silicon Valley.

Says President Leshin on the institute's website, "WPI, a technological university with a human heart and a global reach, approaches STEM learning and discovery the way it should be approached. It's not good enough to train students in the STEM fields—we expect our students to use their skills to make a positive impact on the world, one project at a time."

Arizona State University

Arizona State University (ASU) created a new program called project-based modular learning (ProMod), which began in the fall of 2015. Students have the option of taking ProMod or taking the traditional educational route, enrolling in seat-based courses.

The program is offered in the following majors: business, digital culture (arts, media, and engineering), kinesiology, life sciences/biology (health and wellness), mechanical engineering, psychology, social work, public service and public policy, sustainability, theater, and tourism development and management.

ProMod allows students to engage in project-based learning all four years of their program. Projects are designed to be interdisciplinary so that students can receive project credits in several different departments at the same time. The ASU says that "through this innovative program, students earn credits that satisfy their general studies and degree requirements; but more importantly, they gain real-world experience and develop a deep understanding of the course material."

In a personal communication on June 24, 2014, Cindy Lietz, associate professor in the School of Social Work and College of Public Service, and Community Solutions associate dean, described to me one project in the School of Social Work. She mentioned Arizona passed SB1208, offering a tuition waiver to young adults ages twenty-three or younger who grew up in foster care. Despite the benefit of this effort, many former foster youth are unaware of the waiver. Those who are aware often become overwhelmed by the application process, and those who do apply and are accepted to ASU are often unprepared for higher education.

The purpose of the ProMod project is to recruit and retain former foster youth at ASU. Students that enroll in this one-year ProMod project will work in groups to develop projects that will target recruitment or retention.

This project not only includes designing methods to achieve the desired outcomes but also entails writing papers, giving speeches, learning the ethics of social work research, and completing sixty hours of fieldwork with community agencies. In addition, students learn other corollary skills, such as collaboration, responsibility, time management, and creativity.

Projects vary in complexity. Some are smaller and are completed in a semester, whereas others are more in-depth and may take longer than a year to complete. Elizabeth D. Phillips, provost emeritus and professor of psychology at ASU, and designer of the ProMod program, mentioned that ASU has a fairly significant population of minorities and first-generation college students. And she believes ProMod is a more effective method of engaging students in their learning.

Discussing what she thought the main benefits of this method were, Phillips said, "Project-based learning is more engaging for the students, and they learn better with this method. Students are more motivated because the learning is meaningful and they care about their performance" (personal communication, June 19, 2015).

There are other colleges using project-based learning in some of their departments and programs, but they are much more limited in scope than the colleges mentioned above. One is more likely to find project-based learning in college STEM programs than in other departments. Project Kaleidoscope, for example, is a branch of the Association of American Colleges and Universities, with the purpose of providing STEM faculty with professional-development opportunities to become more innovative. They offer opportunities to learn about projects that can effectively engage students in real-world learning.

HIGH SCHOOLS USING PROJECT-BASED

EdVisions

EdVisions, Inc., is a leading organization that helps hi
project-based learning in their curriculums; however, the
for students. Their focus is entirely student-centered, wl
and develop their own projects, which increases motivaciuii to icaiii. i iicii
flagship school is called Minnesota New Country School (MNCS), located in
Henderson, Minnesota.

Jim Wartman, one of the lead teachers at this school, explained to me the
importance of using a student-centered philosophy with this approach:

> Students have to be given choice in the way they direct their learning. The
> advisor needs to take an approach of listening and facilitating a brainstorming
> session; they are then taking the correct role as a supporter. The advisor can sug-
> gest resources, connect them to community experts, and help them find tools.
>
> Through this empowering approach students gain the confidence to become
> self-directed learners. Over time their confidence grows, they take more risks,
> and the quality and scope of their work becomes limitless. When that is flipped
> around—teacher as director—students lose interest. The student then becomes
> the entity that checks off the boxes and goes through the motions. With the
> teacher as project leader the student does not have to use their creativity, solve
> problems, or put themselves in the position of risk taking. (Personal communi-
> cation, June 18, 2015)

Wartman believes students should be allowed to make mistakes, because
that is how people learn, and that teachers should act as guides to the learning
process and allow students to take responsibility for their learning. He also
mentioned the true value in this approach is that, over time, students switch
their thinking and realize they are responsible for their own learning, especially those who came from traditional school settings where teachers direct
the learning process and where students are forced to listen and memorize
information. He mentioned that this switch in thinking for students does
not happen right away and that educators have to be patient; but he says if
the educator stays the course, most students will learn how to become self-
directed learners.

When visiting MNCS, one immediately notices that the school looks much
different than a traditional high school. The main room is large, without
walls, and contains several clusters of computers.

Each cluster or pod has ten to twelve computers in a semi-circle with work-
station desks. The large room looks more like a business office than a classroom, where some people are busy working at their own workstations, and

are walking around talking with each other about how to solve differ-
problems they are facing while in the process of completing their projects.

One room contains several pieces of woodworking machinery, and while
visiting I noticed a number of wood duck boxes the students had built that
were stacked up against the wall. One of the teachers mentioned that they
would hang them ten feet above the ground on trees where the wood ducks
could nest and be free from predators.

They hung the duck boxes at a local nature center, which students visited
frequently to do research projects. Another room in the school is a green-
house, home to various carnivorous plants that students research and several
fish tanks filled with different specimens also used for research purposes.

When speaking to students, one gets the impression that they behave and
talk more like college students than their high school peers. One particular
student was building a full-size smart board for the school. He explained how
he was using laser technology in the board. Another student was building a
water fountain for the school, and yet another explained that he was working
on designing computer software programs.

The school looked more like a graduate-level classroom, where students
were busy researching ideas on their computers, discussing ideas with peers
and advisors, and collaborating with peers while constructing various projects. They were excited and enthusiastic about their work because it was
relevant and meaningful to them.

Students were extremely interested in their own projects and were excited
to explain intricate details of their projects. It did not take long to realize that
these students were very motivated about learning because they were working
on projects that they were interested in and because they will integrate them
into the school or community where fellow students will have access to them.

At MNCS, project-based learning is at the heart of the curriculum. Students
create their own projects and are assessed on their learning, primarily during
the presentation phase of the project process. Projects are the curriculum, and
books are used to help students design and create their projects.

Textbooks are viewed as tools that can help students move forward in
gathering necessary information needed to complete their projects. If the
advisory group—consisting of advisors, parents, community members, and
peers—agrees that the student has reached a certain level of proficiency, then
they sign off on the project, and the student moves on to the next project.

Much of the time students work alone on their own projects, primarily
because of their own specific interests; however, students are allowed to
collaborate when they have similar interests on a project. Projects are broad
ranging and have included things like designing museums, developing software programs, creating videos and movies, and creating documentaries
through pictures (Newell 2003).

Depending on their complexity, these projects may take a few days or several months to complete. When students finish a project, they demonstrate their level of understanding by doing a formal presentation for their advisory group.

After the presentation, advisors and students sit down together and discuss what state curriculum standards have been met and how many credits the student will receive for their work. However, if the group agrees that the student did not complete the work satisfactorily, the student must continue to work on the project and present it again to their advisory group.

In the state of Minnesota, students must complete all state standards. Students at EdVision's schools are provided a copy of the standards when they enroll at the school and are asked to be mindful of how they might complete these standards through their projects.

Students move through this process at their own pace and finish their high school education when they have met all the mandatory state standards. Advisors work closely with students to make sure that all standards have been met through their project work. Some students graduate earlier than their traditional counterparts, and others graduate later.

In 2006, WestEd was commissioned to conduct research for the US Department of Education on charter schools that were closing the achievement gap. The publication that resulted from this research is titled *Charter High Schools Closing the Achievement Gap* (WestED 2006). Researchers found that MNCS was one of the top eight charter schools in the nation in closing the achievement gap.

In 2005, MNCS had 24 percent of their students qualify for special education services compared to 12 percent at the neighboring high school, LeSueur Henderson Secondary School (LHSS). Even though MNCS had higher numbers of special education students, they outperformed LHSS, scoring 80 percent proficiency in math compared with 73 percent for LHSS students. In addition, MNCS students' average ACT scores were 23.3 compared with a national average of 20.9 (WestEd 2006, 46).

The project process at MNCS from beginning to end includes writing a project proposal, getting approval from the advisor, presenting the proposal to the proposal team, working on the project until it is completed, meeting with the proposal team to determine what standards have been met, and presenting the project to the proposal team. Figure 6.1 provides more detail on how students walk through the project process at MNCS.

Project Foundry is an online software program used at MNCS that helps students progress through their projects in a structured fashion and allows advisors to track the students' progress. The software program provides a variety of forms that students fill out as they reach certain steps in the project

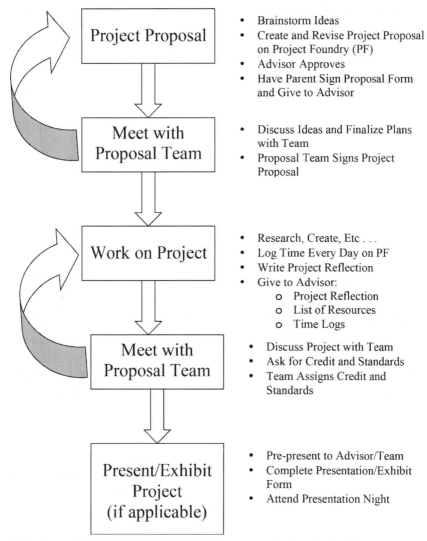

Figure 6.1.   The Life Cycle of a Project at Minnesota New Country School

process. It also helps determine what standards and benchmarks are met with each project.

High Tech High

High Tech High is a high school and college all rolled up together. It is a charter school that uses project-based learning extensively, but it also offers

teacher licensure and two master's degree programs. They launch
charter school in 2000 and currently operate eleven lottery charte
San Diego County.

The concept behind the school, according to its website, wa:
by forty high-tech industry leaders who came together because uiey were
concerned about the lack of individuals, especially women and minorities,
who were qualified to work in the high-tech industry. The first school, Gary
and Jerri-Ann Jacobs' High Tech High, was a success, and ten more schools
have since opened.

High Tech High is unique in that it not only has created multiple charter
schools but it also has created its own teacher credentialing program and
started a new graduate school of education complete with master's degree
programs in teacher leadership and school leadership. Educators can work
on their own professional development through these degree programs while
working at a High Tech High.

There are four design principles that these schools operate under: personalization, adult world connection, common intellectual mission, and teacher
as designer. The education is personalized because students design and create
projects that are of interest to them, with advisors helping guide them through
the learning process. Students do internships and projects in the community
during their junior and senior years, which connects them to adults in the
community.

There is a common mission to help students develop life skills and prepare
them for college and technical education so they can be successful in the
work world after graduation. Teachers work in teams to design and implement interdisciplinary lessons that help students connect ideas from one class
to the next.

The learning process focuses mostly on project-based learning; however,
students have opportunities to do internships out in the community. The
project-based learning process is teacher-directed. However, it is always a
goal to tap into the interest of the students so that they are engaged and motivated to learn.

While discussing High Tech High's teacher training program with Ben
Daley, chief academic officer, I asked him two questions: How do you think
teacher preparation programs should be training teachers to teach in your
schools, and what does your organization do to prepare teachers to teach in
your schools?

Daley mentioned that he has interviewed hundreds of teachers over the
years and recognizes that many teachers find that their teacher preparation
program lacked enough grounding in practice to apply the information they
learned from their schooling. For the most part, programs do not cover any

information on project-based learning. Teachers come to High Tech High lacking an understanding of how to use innovative teaching approaches that engage students in this methodology.

Educators also seem to lack the ability to apply the methods and techniques they learned in their programs because they were not provided enough opportunities to apply information immediately after learning it. Teacher preparation programs tend to emphasize theoretical concepts but are lacking in practical applications. Teacher candidates told him that much of their course work was not relevant and that they had to learn how to use new teaching methodologies at High Tech High.

High Tech High prepares teachers to teach in their schools by offering their own teacher licensure program. This organization hires individuals they believe fit their school model and trains them while they are teaching on site.

It is similar to on-the-job training programs, except that many of High Tech High's teachers have an educational background in teaching and learning. Daley gave me an example of how they hired a PhD in biology who did not have teacher licensure, but this individual became a successful teacher at High Tech High after going through their program.

High Tech High's teacher program is designed such that teachers can take coursework once a week in the evenings and immediately apply the information in their classrooms. There is no lag time between theory and application.

In many traditional teacher-preparation programs, students learn theories and techniques but are not provided opportunities to apply the information until they do their student teaching, which usually occurs in the fourth or fifth year of the program. High Tech High's program requires two years of coursework and culminates with a portfolio highlighting all the competencies required by the State of California for the applicant to become a fully licensed teacher.

In addition, High Tech High has created a master's degree program in teacher leadership and another in school leadership. The teacher leadership program is for teachers who want to continue their professional development and learn cutting-edge theories and techniques that will help them become more effective teachers.

The school leadership degree is for individuals who desire to become administrators in schools. Both programs are two years in length with coursework occurring in the evenings. These programs emphasize a concept called "putting it to practice," which is similar to their teacher licensure program, in that these individuals immediately apply what they are learning as teachers and future administrators.

Each program has its own set of requirements. The teacher leadership program requires students to do an action research project, where teachers identify a problem to solve in their classroom and, through the action-research model, identify a problem, conduct research on the problem, and work toward a resolution.

The school leadership program requires individuals to do a leadership project, create a leadership philosophy statement, and create a school design plan. Individuals in this program are also required to spend a full year in a school working under a school administrator mentor (personal communication, July 1, 2015).

Big Picture Learning

In 1995 Dennis Littky and Elliot Washor started Big Picture Learning with the purpose of creating schools that focused on engaging students in their learning by providing them with relevant hands-on experiences in their communities. In 1996 they created the Metropolitan Regional Career and Technical Center, which has since received considerable notoriety because of its unique approach to educating one student at a time, placing them in the community doing internships and projects that benefit both the student and partnering organization. Currently there are over sixty Big Picture schools in the United States. These schools are based on ten distinguishers, according to the program's website, which must all work together in order for students to be successful:

 1. Learning in the real world: LTI
 2. One student at a time: Personalization
 3. Authentic assessment
 4. School organization
 5. Advisory structure
 6. School culture
 7. Leadership
 8. Parent/family engagement: Adult support
 9. School/college partnership: College preparation and support
10. Professional development

The heart of the learning process at Big Picture schools is learning through internships—or LTIs. This is where students, through the help of their advisors, identify an internship that they are interested in pursuing, contact a mentor from the organization, and determine the specifics of the internship.

During the internship experience, students complete one major project and conduct an exhibition at the end of the internship where they do a formal presentation of what they learned during the internships. Students have a variety of other learning activities they are engaged in during school days; however, internships are the centerpiece to learning at these schools (Littky and Grabelle 2004).

In a phone conversation with Elliot Washor, codirector of Big Picture Learning, I asked whether teachers were prepared to teach at Big Picture schools. He thought teacher candidates spend way too much time in classroom-based courses steeped in theory and lacking in practice. He believes that teacher-preparation programs should have their students in classroom settings as much as possible to expose them to the realities of teaching.

He mentioned that teacher candidates need to be in the classroom every day, observing and experiencing what they will be doing after they graduate from the program. They need to be immersed in the schools, surrounded by students, teachers, mentors, administrators, and families associated with the school where they wish to do their student teaching.

Professors in teacher preparation programs spend too much time discussing theories and techniques foreign to the candidates, Washor believes. Candidates will not understand the theories and techniques until they are engaged in the practice of teaching.

He suggests that teacher preparation programs hold classes after the typical school day and that these classes be used as a mechanism for candidates to discuss and reflect on what they experienced during the school day. Direct experience is key to learning how to teach, and until programs figure this out, candidates will graduate without much understanding of how to teach at these innovative schools.

Big Picture Learning does not have a teacher certification program, although they have had discussions about creating one. They do have teacher-training programs in the summer as well as during the school year. They attempt to find individuals who will perform well as teachers in their system and then educate them to teach according to the Big Picture educational philosophy.

Washor mentioned Big Picture schools provide coaches and mentors to new teachers to help them become adjusted to the school. Individuals that have been exposed to using experiential learning models tend to adjust much more quickly to their philosophy than individuals coming from traditional teacher-preparation programs. He also mentioned that individuals exposed to service learning with an entrepreneurial flare also seem to adjust much more quickly than others.

Expeditionary Learning

Although the concepts behind expeditionary learning were initiated in 1987 when the Harvard Outward Bound Project joined forces with the Harvard

Graduate School of Education to increase academic rigor with Outward Bound's work in schools, the first expeditionary schools were not created until 1993. Ten schools were selected in five cities: New York, Boston, Denver, Portland, and Dubuque, according to Expeditionary Learning's website. These schools were created from a New American Schools Development Corporation $9 million grant. Since that time, Expeditionary Learning has helped create over 150 schools across the country.

Their schools are modeled on five core practices that each school must agree to follow and implement in order to be called an Expeditionary Learning school (per their website):

1. Learning expeditions: Addressing standards through project-based curriculum connecting to real-world need
2. Active pedagogy: Infusing dynamic instructional practices that build skills and critical thinking
3. Culture and character: Building a schoolwide culture of trust, respect, responsibility, and joy in achievement
4. Leadership and school improvement: Strengthening leadership across the school in instruction, culture, and curriculum
5. Structures: Creating time for student and adult learning, collaboration, and focus on excellence

Learning expeditions are the centerpiece of their curriculum and are created by the teachers. Learning expeditions are usually six to twelve weeks in length and require students to acquire skills in reading, writing, listening, speaking, research, critical thinking, problem solving, and collaboration.

Learning expeditions require students to follow a certain process, which includes formulating guiding questions, selecting case studies, and designing projects and products that include working in the field with experts to do service learning. Service learning projects in the community are often the culminating experiences for expeditions, which benefits both the community and the students.

For example, students might partner with a local Department of Natural Resources office to test water samples from a local stream to determine how to improve water quality. This might require students to do presentations at a town hall meeting to discuss their findings and explain ways to reduce stream pollutants.

The result might be a service learning project where students and community members implement a plan to reduce these pollutants. Like some of the other school models mentioned in this section, projects can be small or big, requiring a week or several months to complete.

Scott Hartl, Expeditionary Learning CEO, mentioned to me that there were three skills his new teachers lack. First of all, Teachers in Expeditionary Learning schools lack an understanding of how to implement formative assessments where they can identify short-term and long-term learning goals and understand how to track student progress while students are attempting to meet their goals.

Assessing a learning expedition, which may include completing a semester-long project, requires teachers to broaden their thinking on how and what to assess during this process. A multiple-choice test will provide a summative assessment, but it is much more challenging to assess life skills like critical thinking and responsibility while creating and conducting a project.

A second skill that is lacking is the teacher's ability to creatively apply academic standards to learning expeditions. Teachers must be able to mesh academic standards with learning expeditions because students must meet all academic standards prior to graduating from EL schools.

Teachers need to understand the standards and be able to apply them to unique learning experiences at EL schools. Assessing students' knowledge while they are creating a community garden, for example, requires teachers to think about how science or English standards can be met through this experience.

Third and finally, pedagogical delivery of the standards in EL schools requires teachers to have a thorough understanding of how to engage students in projects that will allow them to apply information over a long period of time. Teachers need to understand that mastery of skills requires a continuous process where students are allowed, on an ongoing basis, to apply what they are learning. Teachers need to allow students to go through numerous trial-and-error attempts in order for students to learn how to problem solve and think critically.

When asked what his organization does to prepare teachers to teach in his schools, Hartl said one of the primary functions of EL is professional development for teachers. Teachers wishing to work at an EL school can attend a number of institutes hosted by EL, which also provides coaches who will come to a school and mentor teachers on the EL process.

New Tech Network

Local business leaders were concerned about creating a school that would help students develop important skills that would allow them to succeed in college and the workplace, and after many discussions the first New Tech School, called the Napa New Tech High School, began operation in 1996. The success of this first school led to a $6 million grant from the Bill and Melinda Gates Foundation, which allowed New Tech to launch fourteen more schools. The New Tech Network supports over 160 schools in twenty-five states, according to their website.

Their school model focuses on three primary ideas: the use of project-based learning, the use of smart technology, and creating a culture of trust, respect, and responsibility. Project-based learning allows students to work together on relevant projects, which helps enhance their motivation to learn. All the classrooms are equipped with a one-to-one computer ratio for students.

This allows students to rely less on teachers and become researchers as they find necessary information to create and build their projects. Finally, New Tech Schools foster an atmosphere of trust and respect by having students work together on projects and be responsible to their peers by completing individual tasks necessary to completing the group project.

Project-based learning is at the core of the learning process. Students have the freedom to do their research on their own computers, and the teachers act as guides in the learning process.

Most projects require collaboration from all students as they work toward completing their group projects. Students at New Tech high schools learn important life skills like responsibility, communication, and teamwork.

New Tech High has an interesting approach to training teachers. They believe that in order to prepare teachers to use project-based learning, entire schools and districts need to be educated on how to use this process. School districts work with New Tech Network for up to a year before the opening of a school. In this planning year, stakeholders including district, school, community, and business leaders visit exiting New Tech schools to see and experience the pervasive transformation in school culture and instructional pedagogy across a school campus.

They believe that the transformation in instruction and the development of college- and career-ready students is built on a highly personalized process that empowers students and teachers. Much of New Tech's training and support is focused on building school cultures and creating systems on a school campus that will allow all teachers to develop and implement standards-based projects throughout the school year.

In a July 6, 2015 conversation with Tim Presiado, senior director of New School development, I learned that teachers and administrators experience a variety of training leading up to the opening of a New Tech school; this includes leadership training for NT principals, shadowing for teachers in exiting NT schools, a five-day training session in the summer that focuses on project-based learning, the deep integration of technology, and the development of school culture. A hallmark of all New Tech training is that the New Tech Network uses the project-based learning process in all of their events to put teachers and administrators in the role of student. This allows the New Tech facilitators and coaches to model the project-based learning process and enables the participants to experience this pedagogical approach firsthand.

PROJECT-BASED LEARNING AT ALL LEVELS OF EDUCATION

The colleges and schools mentioned above are exemplary institutions that have intentionally integrated project-based learning through much of their curriculum. There are many other schools and colleges using project-based learning but not necessarily to the same extent. When project-based learning is less teacher-directed and more student-centered, students learn to tap into their interests and create projects that are relevant to them.

They learn skills such as self-direction, time management, responsibility, organization, and public speaking. They also learn how to problem solve because projects require a process of trial and error. Students try something, and if it does not work they must think of a different plan and try it again. They find solutions through a process of thinking and doing and learn to solve problems by testing out their ideas against reality.

This approach can be used in traditional college and school settings, but educators must create a different culture in the classroom where students are given time to research and collect information that they need to complete their projects. This will require students to do research, possibly make visits to places in the community, and spend time in the library or computer lab. They need freedom to collect necessary information in order to complete their projects.

Conclusion

Educational systems are beginning to slowly change. More and more colleges are recognizing the value of competency-based education and are beginning to implement programs that use project-based learning; and in some cases entire colleges are using competency-based education models. At the high school level, reform organizations are replicating schools across the country that utilize project-based learning and other experiential approaches to learning. Educators are using it in their learning environments because they observe firsthand that it motivates and excites students to learn.

Educators need courage to take the necessary steps to implement project-based learning into their classes, but once they make this transition they will understand why it is a more effective teaching approach. This will not be easy, especially if they are accustomed to using more traditional teaching approaches, but in order to motivate students and keep them excited about learning, educators must learn how to use it in their classrooms. Without motivation, very little significant learning ever occurs.

Parents want their children to learn life skills, and employers want to hire graduates that have these skills, yet many educators continue to use outdated teaching methods that result in apathy and boredom. We are a society that wants to see immediate results, and this may be one reason why the education system continues to cling to the lecture method followed by bubble tests.

Test scores are immediate, and they provide numbers that are easy to understand. But if the education system is going change for the better, policymakers, administrators, and educators must realize that developing life skills is a long, slow process that occurs when students are given the freedom to pursue their interests and are given ample time to work on in-depth projects that often take numerous trial-and-error attempts before completion. Through this process, students learn important life skills that they can carry with them throughout their lives.

LEADERSHIP

Individuals in leadership positions in higher education have tremendous influence over what happens in both higher education and high school classrooms. College administrators can influence what happens in higher-education classrooms and can help influence the types of assessments implemented at their colleges. Performance-based assessments need to replace the traditional bubble tests that are still commonly used for assessment purposes. Demonstrating what students know is much more valuable and effective than memorizing information for exams.

Individuals in leadership positions must understand that project-based learning can be implemented in any classroom environment but requires time to educate instructors on how to effectively use it. Many universities and colleges have teaching and learning centers that provide professional development for their faculty, and these are excellent venues to promote the use of project-based learning.

Instructors need to understand that when students are allowed to pursue their interests through in-depth projects the learning is deep, relevant, and meaningful. However, students need time to complete these projects and present them to their peers, which helps strengthen the learning.

CLASSROOM CULTURE

The culture in classrooms must switch from teacher-directed to student-centered. Educators need to release some control and provide more freedom, provided that students are working toward their goal of completing the project.

Students need freedom to move around the classroom—and, for that matter, around the campus and community—to conduct their research so they can move forward in completing their projects. Structure through the use of forms, artifacts, and learning logs is necessary with project-based learning, but no longer should students be confined to their chairs passively listening to the instructors lecture.

A culture in which students attempt multiple trial-and-error episodes in order to complete their projects must be the norm. Students must not be immediately handed the answers to their questions but instead should be made to test out their ideas against reality to discover answers on their own.

This is a challenging process that requires that they learn through their failures. This type of classroom culture treats them like adults and allows them freedom to grow and learn through direct experience, which is the process professionals engage in on a daily basis when they are in their work environments.

CREATING PROJECTS

Before implementing project-based learning, instructors need to consider several issues. For instance, who should create the project—the student or the instructor? When students create their own projects, they tend to take more ownership because it was their idea and not the instructor's, and, therefore, they take a strong interest in completing it.

When instructors create the projects, there is a possibility that students might not take an interest in the topic. However, when several options are presented and students are allowed to choose one, then they tend to take more interest in it.

Working alone or in groups is another important consideration because there are advantages and disadvantages to each. Working alone, for example, allows students to choose their own projects that are of greater interest to them, but they are not learning how to work as a team with other group members.

Conversely, working in groups allows students the opportunity to learn collaboration skills, but the project may not be of particular interest to certain individuals in the group. It may be beneficial to offer the option of both individual and group projects in the same course so they have opportunities to create their own projects, as well as to work together with their peers. It might be beneficial to have students do one project with a group and another on their own in the same course. Feedback from my course evaluations suggest that they enjoy the opportunity to work on two different projects.

SKILLS

In large lecture halls, one can observe on a daily basis college students in the back rows using their phones and laptops to text and engage in social media. Some students in the very back rows might even be sleeping. In some cases, undergraduate students rarely attend any classes at all and yet receive passing grades simply because they have acquired the notes necessary to do well on tests. What are students learning in these classes?

then CORE

Engagement is the first step toward learning, and when students are allowed to do projects that are of interest to them they become motivated and inspired to learn something. What is extremely interesting is that when students are engaged in project-based learning they are often unaware that they are learning life skills such as the ones discussed in this book. Parents and employers want students to learn these skills, so educators should use this method because it promotes skill development.

The primary skill students appear to be learning is memorization. This skill is not a bad one, but there are others that are equally if not more important. Research continues to tell us that the skills students need to be successful in their professions, and in life in general, are not being taught.

Graduates enter the work world unprepared to take on challenging tasks and projects. These skills must be fostered in our schools and colleges so students graduate with the ability to collaborate and be creative problem solvers.

PROOF

In today's world, administrators usually want scientific proof that something works before they will consider implementing it in their school or college. The research on this topic is thick at both the college and K–12 levels. Chapter 3 provided multiple empirical research studies at both levels that can be used as proof that it results in multiple benefits for both students and educators.

Teacher acceptance occurred in one study after they started using project-based learning and observed how it engaged students in their learning. Project-based learning has benefits that include increased motivation, increased self-confidence, enhanced life skills development, and increased content knowledge.

It has also shown to be effective with underachieving students as well as advanced students. At the collegiate level, it was shown to be effective with nontraditional returning students as well as traditional-age undergraduate students.

PROJECTS AND PLACE

With a little creativity, educators can turn their place into projects. Universities, colleges, schools, and communities always have needs that are unmet. Some needs are small, and others are large, so educators may need to help students craft their projects at the outset so that they are able to complete them by the end of the course; nonetheless, project opportunities are endless.

Projects can help address these needs and when completed can help improve the organization. Students are highly capable of identifying some of these needs, but educators and students can also reach out to organizations and ask them what types of projects would improve their work environments.

Projects can be local, or they can be global. Instructors can talk with administrators at their college or school and inquire about their needs. This way, instructors can offer ideas for potential projects to students at the outset of the course.

Projects can also be global, where students reach out to individuals and organizations from faraway places to help them design and complete projects. Digital technology now allows students to readily communicate with people from afar to design and build projects.

TRACKING AND ASSESSING

Students need structure that will help them continue moving forward in the project process, but too much structure may become unnecessary busywork that slows them down in their learning. Forms and artifacts are key to helping them solidify their project ideas, but don't overdo it on the paperwork. Forms are to be used in order for students to build upon their ideas as they move through the process toward project completion.

Studies on assessing project-based learning have also shown that it enhances academic development. The assessment process is considerably different than the traditional method of test taking. Students demonstrate what they know by presenting their projects to peers and teachers.

This process clearly reveals whether students understand the content or not. In many cases, students are asked to clarify different pieces of their projects and continue working on them until they have completed the project to a satisfactory level.

Presentations are critical to the project process and should be incorporated into class time as often as possible. Presentations are where students demonstrate their knowledge of the project by expressing how they created it and the process they went through to complete it. Standing up in front of peers and talking about their projects helps them develop important communication skills and provides an opportunity for them to overcome their fears of public speaking.

This assessment process mirrors reality because this is often how projects get completed at the workplace. Why not engage students in this process while in school, providing them with experiences that will help them become effective professionals after they graduate?

INCREASING NUMBERS

The education system in the United States is beginning to make a shift to more student-centered classrooms. There is still plenty of talk about the testing craze, but policymakers, administrators, and educators are beginning to realize that learning models focusing on competency-based education and deeper learning are more effective at inspiring students to learn and at assessing what really matters.

The pendulum appears to be swinging from more passive methods of learning to more active methods. Educators are using more experiential approaches to learning—especially project-based learning.

More and more schools are implementing it on a broad scale and attempting to imbed it throughout entire schools and programs. Organizations such as the Competency-Based Education Network, the Council for Adult and Experiential Learning, The Association for Experiential Education, Hewlett Foundation's Deeper Learning Network, and the Buck Institute for Education are pushing for more experiential learning and in particular project-based learning.

Research articles, books, and conferences are growing in number on this topic, and the term *project-based learning* is appearing in more mainstream education journals. This is the dawn of a new era in education, where students will become more active participants in their learning and educators will become guides of the learning process, focusing on helping students learn important skills that they will use the rest of their lives.

Finally, I have been teaching in higher education since 1992 and know one thing for sure: project-based learning works. Students love to be engaged in this type of learning and appreciate opportunities to create and complete relevant, meaningful projects that they can take with them after they graduate and continue to use in their professions. Projects motivate and inspire them to continue learning, and I can't think of a better teaching approach than project-based learning to turn students into lifelong learners.

References

American Federation of Teachers. 2011. "Project Learning Links School with 'After School.'" *American Teacher* 95 (6): 4.

Balcaen, P. 2013. "Attending to Competency Based Education: New Challenges for E-Learning, Pitfalls and Possibilities." In *Proceedings of the Eighth International Conference on e-Learning, Vol. 1*, edited by Eunice Ivala, 24–30. Reading, UK: Academic Conferences and Publishing International Limited.

Barak, M., and Dori, Y. J. 2005. "Enhancing Undergraduate Students' Chemistry Understanding through Project-Based Learning in an IT Environment." *Science Education* 89: 117–39.

Barrell, J. 2007. *Problem-Based Learning: An Inquiry Approach*. Thousand Oaks, CA: Corwin Press.

———. 2010. "Problem-Based Learning: The Foundation for Twenty-First-Century Skills." In *Twenty-First-Century Skills: Rethinking How Students Learn*. Edited by J. Bellanca and R. Brandt, 175–200. Bloomington, IN: Solution Tree Press. Book available online at http://www.nelson.com/pl4u/wp-content/uploads/2015/05/21st CenturySkills_Sample.pdf?e1d0f5.

Barron, B. J., D. L. Schwartz, N. J. Vye, A. Moore, A. Petrosino, L. Zech, and J. D. Bransford. 1998. "Doing with Understanding: Lessons from Research on Problem- and Project-Based Learning." *Journal of the Learning Sciences* 7 (3–4): 271–311.

Barron, K. 2010. "Six Steps for Planning a Successful Project." Edutopia (website), March 15. http://www.edutopia.org/maine-project-learning-six-steps-planning.

Beebe, S. and J. Masterson. 2014. *Communicating in Small Groups: Principles and Practices*. New York: Pearson.

Bender, W. N. 2012. *Project-Based Learning: Differentiating Instruction for the Twenty-First Century*. Thousand Oaks, CA: Corwin.

Blumenfeld, P. C., E. Soloway, R. W. Marx, J. S. Krajcik, M. Guzdial, and A. Palincsar. 1991. "Motivating Project-Based Learning: Sustaining the Doing, Supporting the Learning." *Educational Psychologist* 26 (3–4): 369–98.

Boss, S., J Larmer, and J. Mergendoller. 2013. *PBL for 21st Century Success: Teaching Critical Thinking, Collaboration, Communication, and Creativity.* Novato, CA: Buck Institute for Education.

Butler, T A. 2014. "School Leadership in the Twenty-First Century: Leading in the Age of Reform." *Peabody Journal of Education* 89 (5): 593–602.

Cannon, M., B. Griffith, and J. Guthrie. 2006. *Effective Groups: Concepts and Skills to Meet Leadership Challenges.* New York: Pearson.

Christenson, C., M. Horn, and C. Johnson. 2008. *Disrupting Class: How Disruptive Innovation Will Change the Way the World Learns.* New York: McGraw-Hill.

Cohen, E. and R. Lotan. 2014. *Designing Groupwork: Strategies for the Heterogeneous Classroom.* New York: Teachers College Press.

Cole, J. E., and L. H. Washburn-Moses. 2010. "Going beyond 'The Math Wars': A Special Educator's Guide to Understanding and Assisting with Inquiry-Based Teaching in Mathematics." *Teaching Exceptional Children* 42 (4): 14–21.

Cornell, N., and J. Clarke. 1998. "The Cost of Quality: Evaluating a Standards-Based Design Project." *National Association for Secondary School Principals Bulletin* 83 (603): 91–99.

Dewey, J. 1913. *Interest and Effort in Education.* Ann Arbor, MI: University of Michigan Library.

———. 1938a. *Experience and Education.* New York: Free Press.

———. 1938b. *Logic: The Theory of Inquiry.* New York: Holt, Rinehart, and Winston.

Fullan, M. 2001. *The New Meaning of Educational Change.* New York: Teachers College Press.

Girard, T., M. Pinar, and P. Trapp. 2011. "An Exploratory Study of Class Presentations and Peer Evaluations: Do Students Perceive the Benefits?" *Academy of Educational Leadership Journal* 15 (1): 77–94.

Grant, M., and R. Branch. 2005. "Project-Based Learning in a Middle School: Tracing Abilities through the Artifacts of Learning." *Journal of Research on Technology in Education* 38 (1): 65–98.

Hall, W., S. Palmer, and M. Bennett. 2012. "A Longitudinal Evaluation of a Project-Based Learning Initiative in an Engineering Undergraduate Programme." *European Journal of Engineering Education* 37: 155–65.

Higher Education Research Institute. N.d. *Higher Education Research Institute (HERI) Faculty Survey Compared: 1999 and 2011.* 1–7.

Johnstone, S., and L. Soares. 2014. "Principles for Developing Competency-Based Education Programs." *Change: The Magazine of Higher Learning* 46 (2): 12–19. doi: 10.1080/00091383.2014.896705.

Jollands, M., L. Jolly, and T. Molyneaux. 2012. "Project-Based Learning as a Contributing Factor to Graduates' Work Readiness." *European Journal of Engineering Education* 37: 143–54.

Jones, E. A., and R. A. Voorhes. 2002. *Defining and Assessing Learning: Exploring Competency-Based Initiatives; Report of the National Postsecondary Education Cooperative Working Group on Competency-Based Initiatives in Postsecondary Education.* With K. Paulson. Washington, DC: NPEC (National Postsecondary Education Cooperative) and US Department of Education. http://nces.ed.gov/pubs2002/2002159.pdf.

Kagesten, O., and J. Engelbrecht. 2007. "Student Group Presentations: A Learning Instrument in Undergraduate Mathematics for Engineering Students." *European Journal of Engineering Education* 32 (3): 202–314.

Kamin, M. 2013. *Soft Skills Revolution: A Guide for Connecting with Compassion for Trainers, Teams, and Leaders.* San Francisco: Pfeiffer.

Kilpatrick, W. H. 1918. "The Project Method." *Teachers College Record* 19, 319–35.

Klein-Collins, R. 2013. "Sharpening Our Focus on Learning: The Rise of Competency-Based Approaches to Degree Completion." National Institute for Learning Outcomes Assessment. Occasional paper #20, 4–19.

Knoll, M. 1997. "The Project Method: Its Vocational Education Origin and International Development." *Journal of Industrial Teacher Education* 34 (3): 59–80.

Krauss, J., and S. Boss. 2013. *Thinking Through Project-Based Learning: Guiding Deeper Inquiry.* Thousand Oaks, CA: Corwin.

Lawrence, E. 2005. *The Peace Seekers: Indian Christians and the Dakota Conflict.* Sioux Falls, SD: Pine Hill Press.

Lenz, B., J. Wells, and S. Kingston. 2015. *Transforming Schools: Using Project-Based Learning, Performance Assessment, and Common Core Standards.* San Francisco: Jossey-Bass.

Levine, E. 2002. *One Kid at a Time: Big Lessons from a Small School.* New York: Teachers College Press.

Littky, D., and S. Grabelle. 2004. *The Big Picture: Education Is Everyone's Business.* Alexandria, VA: Association for Supervision and Curriculum Development.

Liu, M., and Y. Hsiao. 2002. "Middle School Students as Multimedia Designers: A Project-Based Learning Approach." *Journal of Interactive Learning Research* 13 (4): 311–37.

Markham, T., J. Larmer, and J. Ravitz. 2003. *Project-Based Learning Handbook: A Guide to Standards Focused Project-Based Learning for Middle and High School Teachers.* Novato, CA: Buck Institute for Education.

Martinez, M. R., and D. McGrath. 2014. *Deeper Learning: How Eight Innovative Public Schools Are Transforming Education in the Twenty-First Century.* New York: The New Press.

Mintz, S. 2015. "Competency-Based Education 2.0." Inside Higher Ed (blog), February 22. https://www.insidehighered.com/blogs/higher-ed-beta/competency-based-education-20.

Movahedzadeh, F., R. Patwell, J. Rieker, and T. Gonzalez. 2012. "Project Based Learning to Promote Effective Learning in Biotechnology Courses." *Education Research International* 1–8, DOI: 10.1155/2012/536024

Newell, R. 2003. *Passion for Learning: How Project-Based Learning Meets the Needs of Twenty-First-Century Students.* Lanham, MD: Scarecrow Press.

Newell, R. 2007. *Project-Based Learning.* Unpublished manuscript.

Ordonez, B. 2014. "Competency-Based Education: Changing the Traditional College Degree Power, Policy, and Practice." *New Horizons in Adult Education and Human Resource Development* 26 (4): 47–53.

Palmer, S., and W. Hall. 2011. "An Evaluation of a Project-Based Learning Initiative in Engineering Education." *European Journal of Engineering Education* 36: 357–65.

Pearlman, B. 2006. "New Skills for a New Century." *Edutopia* (June): 50–53. Available online at http://cell.uindy.edu/docs/NewSkillNewCentury.pdf.

Pestallozi, T. 2013. *Life Skills 101: A Practical Guide to Leaving Home and Living on Your Own.* Courtland, OH: Stonewood Publications.

Petkov, D., O. Petkova, and M. D'Onofrio. 2008. "Using Projects Scoring Rubrics to Assess Student Learning in an Information Systems Program." *Journal of Information Systems Education* 19 (2): 241–252.

Pink, D. H. 2009. *Drive.* New York: Penguin Group.

Place-Based Education Evaluation Conference. 2003. *PEEC Overview Paper.* Available online at Http://www.peecworks.org/index.

Quay, S. E., and R. J. Quaglia. 2004. "Creating a Classroom Culture That Inspires Student Learning." *Teaching Professor* 18 (2): 1–2.

Reed, M. K. 2008. "Comparison of the Place Value Understanding of Montessori Elementary Students." *Investigations in Mathematics Learning* 1: 1–27.

Rosen, J. A., E. J. Glennie, B. W. Dalton, J. M. Lennon, and R. N. Bozick. 2010. *Noncognitive Skills in the Classroom: New Perspectives on Educational Research.* Research Triangle Park, NC: RTI Press.

Sander, P., and L. Sanders. 2005. "Giving Presentations: The Impact on Students' Perceptions." *Psychology Teaching Review* 11 (1): 25–39.

Sarkar, S., and R. Frazier. 2008. "Place Based Investigations and Authentic Inquiry." *The Science Teacher* 75 (2): 29–33.

SCANS (Secretary's Commission on Achieving Necessary Skills). 1991. *What Work Requires of Schools: A SCANS Report for America 2000.* Washington, DC: US Department of Labor. Available in part online at http://www.academicinnovations.com/report.html. Available in full at http://wdr.doleta.gov/SCANS/whatwork/whatwork.pdf.

Sinek, S. 2009. *Start with Why: How Great Leaders Inspire Everyone to Take Action.* New York: Penguin Group.

Smith, G. A., and D. Sobel. 2010. *Place- and Community-Based Education in Schools.* Florence, KY: Routledge, Taylor and Francis Group.

Soares, L. 2012. *A "Disruptive" Look at Competency-Based Education: How the Innovative Use of Technology Will Transform the College Experience.* Washington, DC: Center for American Progress. https://cdn.americanprogress.org/wp-content/uploads/issues/2012/06/pdf/comp_based_education.pdf.

Sobel, D. 2005. *Place-Based Education: Connecting Classrooms and Communities.* Great Barrington, MA: The Orion Society.

Starobin, S. S., Y. Chen, A. Kollasch, T. Baul, and F. S. Laanan. 2014. "The Effects of a Preengineering Project-Based Learning Curriculum on Self-Efficacy among Community College Students." *Community College Journal of Research and Practice* 38: 131–43.

Stiggins, R. 2002. "Where Is Our Assessment Future and How Can We Get There from Here?" In R. W. Lissitz and W. D. Schafer, eds. *Assessment in Educational Reform.* Boston, MA: Allyn and Bacon.

Thomas, D., W. Enloe, and R. Newell. 2005. *The Coolest School in America: How Small Learning Communities Are Changing Everything.* Lanham, MD: Scarecrow Education.

Thurneck, L. 2011. "Incorporating Student Presentations in the College Classroom." *Inquiry* 16 (1): 17–30.

Tough, P. 2012. *How Children Succeed: Grit, Curiosity, and the Hidden Power of Character*. New York: Houghton Mifflin Harcourt.

Trilling, B., and C. Fadel. 2009. *Twenty-First-Century Skills: Learning for Life in Our Times*. San Francisco: John Wiley and Sons.

Tucker, B. 2011. "The Truth about Testing Costs." *Education Week* 31 (7): 3.

Wagner, T. 2008. *The Global Achievement Gap*. New York: Basic Books.

Wagner, T. 2012. *Creating Innovators: The Making of Young People Who Will Change the World*. New York: Scribner.

Washor, E., and C. Mojkowski. 2013. *Leaving to Learn: How Out-of-School Learning Increases Student Engagement and Reduces Dropout Rates*. Portsmouth, NH: Heinemann.

WestEd. 2006. *Charter High Schools Closing the Achievement Gap: Innovations in Education*. Washington, DC: US Department of Education. https://www2.ed.gov/admins/comm/choice/charterhs/report.pdf.

Wiggins, G. 1998. *Educative Assessment: Designing Assessment to Inform and Improve Student Performance*. San Francisco, CA: Jossey-Bass.

Wolff, S. J. 2003. *Design Features of the Physical Learning Environment for Collaborative, Project-Based Learning at the Community College Level*. Saint Paul: National Research Center for Career and Technical Education, University of Minnesota.

Wurdinger, S., and J. Carlson. 2009. *Teaching for Experiential Learning: Five Approaches That Work*. Lanham, MD: Rowman and Littlefield.

Wurdinger, S., and W. Enloe. 2011. "Cultivating Life Skills at a Project-Based Charter School." *Improving Schools* 14 (1): 84–96.

Wurdinger, S., and J. L. Rudolph. 2009. "A Different Type of Success: Teaching Important Life Skills through Project-Based Learning." *Improving Schools* 12 (2): 117–31.

Wurdinger, S., and M. Qureshi. 2014. "Enhancing College Students' Life Skills through Project-Based Learning." *Innovative Higher Education* 40 (3): 279–86. doi: 10.1007/s10755-014-9314-3.

Wurdinger, S., J. Haar, R. Hugg, and J. Bezon. 2007. "A Qualitative Study Using Project-Based Learning in a Mainstream Middle School." *Improving Schools* 10 (2): 150–61.

Zhang, K., S. W. Peng, and J. Hung. 2009. "Online Collaborative Learning in a Project-Based Learning Environment in Taiwan: A Case Study on Undergraduate Students' Perspectives." *Educational Media International* 46: 123–35.

Zhou, C. 2012. "Integrating Creativity Training into Problem- and Project-Based Learning Curriculum in Engineering Education." *European Journal of Engineering Education* 37: 488–99.

About the Author

Scott D. Wurdinger is professor of experiential education and leadership studies at Minnesota State University in Mankato, and he currently serves as coordinator of the Educational Leadership Doctoral Program. His research interests focus on the use of various approaches to experiential learning and how experiential learning develops life skills such as critical thinking, problem solving, and creativity. He has been teaching in higher education for the past twenty-four years, and serves as a cadre expert for Innovative Quality Schools, an organization that authorizes charter schools. He enjoys road biking and Nordic skiing in his free time.

Made in the USA
Middletown, DE
31 December 2018